MW00786185

MAINTENANCE AND UPGRADES MANUAL

VW
Classic Beetle

MAINTENANCE AND UPGRADES MANUAL

VW
Classic Beetle

James Peene

THE CROWOOD PRESS

First published in 2022 by
The Crowood Press Ltd
Ramsbury, Marlborough
Wiltshire SN8 2HR

enquiries@crowood.com

www.crowood.com

© James Peene 2022

All rights reserved. No part of this publication may be reproduced or transmitted in any form
or by any means, electronic or mechanical, including photocopy, recording, or any information
storage and retrieval system, without permission in writing from the publishers.

British Library Cataloguing-in-Publication Data
A catalogue record for this book is available from the British Library.

ISBN 978 0 7198 4013 5

Disclaimer
Safety is of the utmost importance in every aspect of an automotive workshop. The practical
procedures and the tools and equipment used in automotive workshops are potentially
dangerous. Tools should be used in strict accordance with the manufacturer's recommended
procedures and current health and safety regulations. The author and publisher cannot accept
responsibility for any accident or injury caused by following the advice given in this book.

Please note that things like timings, plug and points gaps and so on vary depending on year,
model and engine size of the car. Those in this book are generic and correct for the car used
throughout the book. They are also applicable to many, but not every, Beetle; the reader
should consult a model-specific manual for their own vehicle.

Typeset by Simon and Sons

Cover design by Blue Sunflower Creative

Printed and bound in India by Parksons Graphics

Contents

ACKNOWLEDGEMENTS

Producing this book wouldn't have been possible without a little help along the way. A number of trusted friends and specialists were called upon for advice, hints, tips and photographs of their work, so I would like to thank, in no particular order, Alan, Phil and Christine Sutton at Creative Coachworks, Max Edwards at EVA Resto, Alex Noel of Wolfsburg Restos, Georg Otto at CSP, Just Kampers, The VW Engine Company, Jon Gilbert, Steve Gosling, Mark Walker, Paul Knight, Jimbo Wallace, Jon Robinson-Pratt, Joe Dorsey and lastly, but most importantly, Sophie Pinder for putting up with it all.

IMAGE CREDITS

CSP, pages 89 (bottom), 90 (all), 113, 114 (top left, top right, bottom left), 115 (all), 135, 136 (top), 153 (bottom), 155 (bottom), 161 (all), 165 (top); EVA Resto, page 157 (bottom right), 158 (all three in left-hand column); Jimbo Wallace, pages 88 (top and bottom), 89 (top); Jon Gilbert, pages 114 (bottom right), 172, 173 (all); Jon Robinson-Pratt, cover image, pages 24 (bottom right), 60 (all), 61 (all), 62 (all), 154 (top and bottom), 155 (top left and top right); Just Kampers, pages 91 (bottom right), 175; Mark Walker, pages 101 (all), 102 (all), 103 (all), 104 (all), 105 (all); Paul Knight, pages 107 (top left and top right), 111; Steve Parsons, page 7.

Introduction and a Brief History of VW

Having decided to buy, restore or own a VW Beetle, you're in luck. Volkswagen produced over 21million units of the model over the course of a 65-year production run. That's a staggering achievement in anyone's book and one that bodes especially well for the wannabe Beetle owner, as it means there are plenty to choose from and parts availability is absolutely second to none. Forget the likes of your Minis and MGs; if you are looking for a classic car for which you can truly get everything you need to build one from the ground up, a Beetle is the car for you.

German production began in 1938 and officially came to an end in January 1978, when VW switched over to building Golfs, but such was the demand for affordable, reliable transportation in countries like Mexico and Brazil, where countless examples were used as taxis and local transport, that it will come as no surprise to hear that satellite factories continued to turn them out long after the VW mothership had turned its back on air-cooled technology. In fact, the Beetle was only killed off once-and-for-all due to government legislation requiring all Mexican taxis to have four doors. And this measure wasn't specifically aimed at killing the Beetle, but an attempt at reducing crime rates.

Some sections of the motoring press like to claim the Toyota Celica is the best-selling car of all time, but park one of the first and last generation Celicas side-by-side and the only thing they have in common is the name. Park a Beetle from 1938 alongside one of the last ones to roll off the line in 2003 and they are both clearly identifiable as Beetles.

That the Beetle should come to be so universally adored is quite frankly a marvel in itself. It's impossible to talk about the Beetle without mentioning one of the men most instrumental in its birth – a certain Adolf Hitler.

It is ironic that we have one of the worst characters in human history to thank for the Beetle. When the Nazis came to power in 1933, Hitler set out plans to mobilize the masses. He began building the country's *autobahns* and set the wheels in motion for a car to populate them, one that the average worker could afford to buy and run.

The Nazis were the first to popularize the term 'People's Car' and that's what Volkswagen literally translates as when you break the German down into English. Okay, so they also called it the *Kraft-durch-Freude Wagen*, or 'Strength through Joy Car', but after World War II the much friendlier-sounding Volkswagen name was taken up instead.

Land to build the factory was originally commandeered from the Count of Wolfsburg and if you have ever wondered where the Wolfsburg crest on early VWs comes from, now you know. Another name forever linked to the Beetle is Ferdinand Porsche and we all know what he went on to do after coming up with the Beetle…. It was Porsche's design

team that won the contract to design the 'People's Car' and that team also included the likes of Karl Rabe (chief engineer), Josef Kales (engine designer), Erwin Komenda (body specialist) and Josef Mickl and Franz Xaver Reimspiess. The latter also came up with the iconic VW badge.

There was even a savings scheme to help would-be owners buy their Beetle. Pay five German marks a month and receive a stamp in a savings booklet. When you had enough stamps you would receive your car, but sadly no one ever did. World War II came along and the factory began producing military vehicles such as the Beetle-based Kübelwagen and Schwimmwagen instead.

Understandably, the VW factory was heavily bombed throughout the war and that really should have been it for Volkswagen. However, when the victorious Allies divided Germany up after the war, Wolfsburg was located in an area that fell under British control. A British Army Officer, Major Ivan Hirst of the Royal Electrical and Mechanical Engineers (REME), took control of what remained of the bombed-out ruins of the factory and, to cut a long story short, was directly responsible for getting the Beetle back into production.

Hirst discovered that the Beetle presses had escaped the Allied bombing, and with post-war Europe in dire need of transportation he decided the Beetle would be

The Volkswagen factory in Wolfsburg, Germany.

a welcome addition to the market. A pre-war Beetle was pulled from the ruins, painted khaki green and sent up to the British HQ in Germany for evaluation. The top brass liked the look of it so placed an initial order for 20,000 to be built, thus safe-guarding the immediate future of the factory.

However, there is one man more than any other whom we have to thank for turning VW into an automotive colossus – Heinz Nordhoff. He became the General Manager of VW in January 1948. Between then and his death in 1968, Nordhoff oversaw what is now regarded as the golden age of VW. He took the Beetle to hither-to undreamt of heights, green-lighting the Type 2 Transporter for production, as well as the Type 3 family and Karmann Ghia. Nordhoff also built up a vast network of dealerships and created factories all over the world, but none of that would have been possible if it hadn't been for the humble little car we came to know as the Beetle.

As a result of being built in such vast quantities, there are still a ton of NOS (New Old Stock) parts for Beetles to be

> ### GLOBAL SUCCESS
>
> The Beetle wasn't just built in Germany. Such was its success that VW set up satellite factories all around the world to build them, either in their entirety or in kit form using parts shipped out from the mother factory. Hence, you can buy Beetles that were assembled in Germany, Brazil, Mexico, Australia, New Zealand, South Africa and even Ireland.

found and thousands of specialists who can sell you newly manufactured parts, fit them for you or restore your car from the ground up should you wish. But where is the fun in having someone do all the hard work for you? By reading this book it is a fair guess that you are already thinking you would like to have a crack at working on a Beetle yourself and that's fantastic. It's easy when you know how, as you are about to discover.

Where to Start?

If you have never worked on a car before but have decided to try your arm with a Beetle, then you're in luck. An air-cooled VW is one of the easiest cars you could have picked to work on. Fact.

Whilst it can seem a daunting task at first, it's actually pretty straightforward taking one apart. Putting it all back together again is, as the old saying goes, simply a reversal of the first process. So as long as you take plenty of pictures on your phone and make a few drawings if needs be, then you should be absolutely fine.

It also really helps to watch as many YouTube videos on whatever job you're planning to tackle as possible and, if possible, talk to a friend who really does know what they're doing and rope them in with the promise of a good laugh, lots of tea or a few beers in the garage. It is also a good idea to join a VW club and visit some of the many Volkswagen shows that are held all over the country throughout the year. They are a fabulous way of amassing the parts you need, as well as for drawing inspiration from other cars.

As a rule, VW owners are a friendly bunch and will cheerfully put a glass eye to sleep once you get them talking about their vehicles and what they've done to them. Make friends with another VW geek and you will find a willing ally – someone who can help you look over a potential purchase, lend you tools and a hand whenever the need arises. You'll find a lot of people come for the cars, but they stay for the scene that surrounds them. You will never be stuck for something to do when you buy a Beetle, that's for sure.

Should the need arise, you can always hand your car over to a specialist to rectify anything that's beyond your capabilities.

TOP: *You don't need to go this far with a Beetle, but they do come apart easily if you want them to. Cars are just a collection of parts – like adult Lego or Meccano.*

GOT TO START SOMEWHERE

What you need to remember is that everyone – no matter how good they are when it comes to wielding the spanners now – had to begin somewhere. You only become proficient at doing something through experience and you will not build any of that up if you're too afraid to have a go yourself.

GETTING STARTED

If this is your first toe in the classic car water, where to start and in what order to tackle things can be a little confusing at first. The best advice on offer is to think about what really needs doing and how urgent any particular job might be. For example, ask yourself if you really need to completely disassemble your car. Does it genuinely need a full strip down, restoration and new paint job?

Blow something apart in your garage and it will be off the road for months – if not years – and there is every chance it may never see the light of day again. If you find this hard to believe, just take a look on a certain internet auction site in the 'unfinished projects' section. It's full of broken dreams, unfulfilled promises and Beetles in boxes.

Carrying out a rolling restoration means that you can continue to drive and enjoy your car whilst steadily improving it over a period of time. Take it from those who know, a huge pile of parts going nowhere in the garage can weigh heavy on your mind, whereas there is no better motivation to see a project through than getting to drive and enjoy your car.

It also really helps if you break a Beetle down into simple, bite-size chunks. A Bug is really just a collection of parts.

There is the main body, which is easily removable once you've disconnected all of the chassis bolts. Then you have the chassis itself, onto which is bolted the front suspension, engine and gearbox. Add on a few sundries like the brakes, fuel lines, wiring and interior and that's really all there is to a Beetle.

What you're going to do with all of those bits and in what order you tackle them is entirely up to you. It may be a case of simply changing the stance and look of the car with some new wheels and suspension upgrades, or you might want to carry out a full nut and bolt, body-off restoration. Either way, you should try to have a clear picture of what you want to achieve before you start taking things apart and then enjoy the process. If you're not enjoying yourself then you're less likely to see your project through to completion – and where's the fun in that?

So, where do you start? Obviously with a car of your own. You may already have a specific year and model in mind; if not, the next chapter should help with that. Then again, you may already own the car you're about to start work on, but it is recommended that you do as much research on the jobs ahead before you begin. Spend as many hours as you like trawling the internet sites and forums. Get a feel for what cars and parts are out there, how much every component and job costs and then add on some contingency money for all the additional work you weren't expecting but will no doubt uncover.

Don't be deterred, but one job always creates another and every twenty-minute job is just one broken bolt away from becoming a three-day nightmare. The flip side of that coin is that working on your own car can also be incredibly therapeutic and rewarding.

There is no better feeling than knowing you have fixed something yourself, even more so when someone asks who did something to your car and you can say: 'I did.'

Know Your Beetle: Year-by-Year Model Changes

Whilst the essential shape of the car remained the same throughout the course of the Beetle's lifetime, there were countless styling changes, mechanical upgrades and little details that make a huge amount of difference to collectors. Here are a few of the main things to look out for so you will know your '63 Beetles from your '73 Beetles when you see one.

SPLIT SCREEN: 1938–1953

This is the first-generation Beetle and so-called because of the two small rear windows. This version is without doubt the most collectable amongst the die-hard enthusiasts, but the cars are also the least useable thanks to things like their 'crash' gearboxes. What that essentially means is there is no synchromesh, so you'll have to acquaint your-

TOP: *A Beetle is not just a Beetle; there are many subtle differences from the first to last models built. How many can you spot here?*

self with the knack of double-declutching or the sound of crunching gears.

Engines in the Split Screen are a feeble affair, with just 25bhp as standard, the electrics run off 6-volts and they have semaphore indicators that today's road users have an alarming tendency to fail to see.

Whilst Splits are the purest form of Beetle, the cars themselves and period correct spares are by far the most expensive to buy, so the first-generation Beetle really isn't for most.

Split Beetles are without doubt truly fabulous cars, upon which the entire VW legend was born, but they are best left to the truly dedicated.

OVAL: 1953–1957

VW chopped the centre section out of the split rear window to create a single, small oval-shaped window, hence cars built in this era are commonly referred to as Ovals. Inside,

It's all about the rear window on a Split – so-called for obvious reasons.

Take the split out of the rear window and you have an Oval.

they have a simplified dashboard; Splits have two exposed gloveboxes but Ovals have only one glovebox, with a metal door and more luxurious upholstery.

You don't get any more creature comforts in an Oval, but driving one is a more pleasurable experience than driving a Split thanks to the introduction of things like part-synchromesh gearboxes, larger 30bhp engines and hydraulic brakes.

Oval lovers will try to convince you that they are the best-quality Beetles ever made, and they do have a point, which makes both the cars and period-correct, quality parts more expensive than later examples. Items such as decent quality wings, doors and bonnets are more expensive than they are for '60s and '70s cars, but they're worth spending money on as a good Oval is hard to beat.

EARLY BIG WINDOW: 1958

Legend has it that towards the end of the 1950s VW approached the Italian design studio Pininfarina and asked what changes they would make to the Beetle; apparently the only suggestion they came back with was to make the rear window larger. That's exactly what VW did in 1957 for

the 1958 model year and hence, these cars are now known as Early Big Window cars. The author's project car is a '58, so has a lot of Oval-era parts and details – for example, the late Oval-style steering wheel, fuel tank and semaphore indicators, but with the larger rear window and a redesigned dashboard that stayed with the Beetle until the end. These are quality machines and easier to live with thanks to their much-improved rear visibility. True enough, their 1192cc 30bhp engines won't set the world alight, but they are sprightly enough, good on fuel and super-reliable if maintained as VW intended.

EARLY BIG WINDOW: 1959–1960

Beetles from this era are pretty much the same as those built for the 1958 model year but no longer have the semaphore indicators mounted in the door pillars. Indicators were added to the tops of the front wings and the rear taillights now flashed. Dashboards remained the same but the Oval-style steering wheels were replaced with a new two-spoke design with a semi-circular horn ring. Exterior door handles are now fixed affairs with push buttons, rather than the hinged ice-pick design of old.

1958 models still retain a lot of cool Oval-era parts.

Small taillights now flash as indicators as the semaphores were deleted. A Golde ragtop sunroof is a highly desirable option.

EARLY BIG WINDOW: 1961–1964

These sport larger rear lights that house separate flashing indicators. They also come with full synchromesh gearboxes and 34bhp engines, which make these later Bugs much nicer to live with on a regular basis. The heating system switched from stale-air to fresh air heat exchangers, so replacement components are cheaper and easier to come by today and fuel gauges were introduced to the dashboard, rather than just being an optional accessory as they were before.

BIG WINDOW: 1965–1966

The Beetle lost some of its cuddly charm for the 1965 model year, as the window size was increased all round. Perhaps confusingly, these are often just referred to as Big Window cars. Optional sunroofs went from being a large folding cloth sunroof to a smaller steel sliding design. As well as the 1200cc engine, you could now get a 1300cc engine. Front suspension was changed from a king- and link-pin setup to ball joint instead. Inside, a central air-vent was added to the dashboard to help with demisting, which was never a particular strong point for any model year of Beetle.

BIG WINDOW: 1967

1967 was a big year for the Beetle and enthusiasts often bang on about cars built in this year, albeit incorrectly. Not all Bugs built in '67 are special, as you could still order a 1200 or 1300 Beetle with drum brakes all round. However, the '67 that gets everyone hot under the collar is the 1500cc model launched for that model year. It had the 1500cc (1493cc) engine and front disc brakes, which necessitated a different style of wheel with cooling slots and flatter hub caps. Electrics went from 6-volt to 12-volt. Engine lids were changed and, whilst the European market retained the prettier, sloping headlights, the US market '67 came with the new style of upright headlights. There are loads of little details that get the '67 fans excited, such as different door locks and valances and so on, but you can wander down that rabbit hole alone.

BIG WINDOW: 1968–1978

These cars are lumped into one category as the final incarnation of the Beetle looked essentially the same, bar some minor changes, until the end of German production. US safety legislation brought styling changes that not everyone agrees were for the best. The early Beetle's much-loved sloping headlights were changed to a more upright design that in turn led to redesigned wings, valances and chunkier, squarer bumpers that are known as Europa bumpers. Even later models had the front indicators relocated to the bumpers rather than on top of the wings. Bonnets and engine lids became shorter, rear lights were increased in size, first for the Tombstone design and then to the Football or Elephant's foot design, so-called for obvious reasons. Engine sizes were 1200, 1300 or 1600cc and all wheels were slotted

The perfect mix of charm and usability, it's hard to beat a Beetle from this era.

Note the larger windows and fatter front indicators.

One year only means year-specific parts are harder to come by.

Big changes here, such as big bumpers and rear lights. Upright headlights, too.

four-bolt steels with flat hubcaps and drum brakes. Chrome trim became smaller and the dashboards eventually lost all traces of bling. Fuel filler flaps were added to the front quarter panel, whereas before you had to open the boot to fill up.

CONVERTIBLES AND RAGTOPS

Throughout the Beetle's lifetime you could order a Cabriolet model. These were made by the coachbuilders Karmann in Osnabrück. Body styles, mechanical components and interiors were aligned with whatever was rolling out of Wolfsburg at the time, but the chassis was strengthened to make up for the loss of roof structure and they came with a snug, leak and draught-free hood. These cars had a full rear seat and windows that rolled down into the rear quarter panels, so don't be fooled by any hack-jobs.

If the full Convertible was too much for you, there was the Golde sunroof option. Up to 1964 this was a folding fabric roof that gave birth to the name 'ragtop'. From '64 onwards the sunroof model was equipped with a steel sliding panel. All of these models command a premium today due to their relative rareness and undoubted cool factor.

1302 AND 1303 SUPER BEETLES

All of the models previously mentioned are known as 'flat-screen Beetles' because of their flat front windscreens. However, VW also offered another type of Beetle, one with a curved, panoramic front windscreen and a more bulbous front end, known as the 1303S. Before that, however, VW launched the 1302 in August 1970. It still had a flat windscreen, but the front end styling was revised to accommodate a different suspension set-up. Regular Beetles all have torsion bar suspension, but the 1302 had MacPherson-strut front ends and independent rear suspension (IRS) at the back. They also had a 1300cc engine and were only produced for two years before VW replaced them with the 1303S. The so-called Big Beetle was powered by a 1600cc engine and along with the bulbous front metal work, now came with the huge, curved windscreen. Inside, they have their own unique style of black plastic Beetle dashboard and whilst they're the least popular model today due to their looks, they're arguably one of the nicest factory-original Beetles to drive and, due to their lack of popularity, bargains can still be had.

The roof goes down and the price goes up. Early Cabriolets and factory-fitted ragtops are some of the most sought-after Beetles today.

Bulbous front end and panoramic front windscreen shouts 1303.

No bonnet trim, painted indicator housings and bumpers scavenged from the parts bin mean only one thing: base model.

Jeans Editions came with black trim and denim seat covers.

BASE MODELS

Known as *Spar Käfers* or Standard models, VW offered these as the budget option to those who didn't want to pony up for a regular Beetle. They were more spartan offerings with less exterior trim (which was often painted rather than chromed), only partial headliners, and were a bit of a parts-bin special that used up the left-over components from outgoing models. For example, whilst in 1973 all regular Beetles came with Europa bumpers and large rear lights, a Base model still had the earlier-style, late 1960s taillights and slim blade bumpers, but without over-riders. They also only had only one sun visor (on the driver's side, not on the passenger's), rubber mats and very basic carpets.

SPECIAL EDITIONS

VW offered a number of Special Edition Beetles to help boost sales over the years. Sun Bugs, Marathon Beetles,

Last Editions, Velvet Editions, Jeans Beetles (with denim upholstery), Triple White Cabriolets, GT Beetles and so on. Don't be fooled into thinking they are any more valuable because of their relative scarcity compared to the rest of the herd and be aware that finding model-specific replacements to restore one back to stock won't be an easy task.

MEXI BUGS

Whilst German production came to an end in January 1978, Beetles continued to be made in VW's Brazil and Mexico factories. A small handful of companies shipped Mexican Bugs into the UK before production finally came to an end in July 2003 and, whilst they have 1600 engines with hydraulic tappets and front disc brakes, they have a reputation for rust. Find a good one that's been well cared for and it will make an excellent and useable daily driver with good parts availability.

Great engines, but Mexican Beetles have a reputation for rust.

Getting the Bug: Viewing and Buying Your Beetle

3

Okay, so you've read the previous chapter and narrowed down which model is for you based on personal preference, intended usage and budget. Of course you haven't. If you're anything even remotely like the author, you've already decided what model and year of Beetle you want and the previous chapter has either justified your choice or you've decided to completely ignore that section anyway. Fair enough.

The one thing you really do need to consider is your budget. This will affect everything that follows, because the absolute best advice is to buy the best example you can afford.

TOP: The golden rule when buying any car is never let your heart rule your head. Even if it's the exact model and colour you have set your heart on, you're better off walking away if the car isn't as good as you had hoped or your budget allows.

This will genuinely save you a huge amount of time and money in the long run, even if you have to save up a bit longer to buy the car you really want and miss out on a few that catch your eye along the way.

Bringing any classic car up to scratch will always consume far more time and money than you budgeted for. Poking around a rusty Beetle is the very definition of opening a can of worms. One job always creates another and there's no such thing as a quick fix, especially if you want your car to last and be reliable.

You are always much better off buying a good car in the first place, then you can add your own personal touches to stamp your mark on it. It might seem counter-intuitive buying a more expensive vehicle, but it's nearly always cheaper than paying to put one right, especially if you can't do all of the work yourself and have to pay others to do it for you.

Whilst this car might look a bit rough around the edges it is an original-paint car, so isn't hiding shoddy repair work. Or so it appeared on first inspection, but you should never judge anything on first sight.

The biggest expense with classic cars of any type is fixing rusty bodywork. Rust repair is a time-consuming and therefore expensive undertaking. To repair rotten sections properly, you have to chop out the rust, buy or make replacement sections, weld them in, tidy them up, prep and paint them. On the other hand, replacing worn-out mechanical components is (usually) as straightforward as removing a broken item and bolting on its replacement. Hence, it is always recommended to buy a mechanically tired car with a decent body rather than a rusty one that appears to run well.

By now you're probably itching to know what and where to check on a Beetle. It's fundamentally the same on any Beetle – no matter that the year and age is not always an indication of how good something is. For example, a well-looked after '60s car can be a more solid proposition than an unloved '70s example.

It is a commonly held believe that earlier cars were better made than later examples, as VW used thicker metals and higher grade materials. True or not, always buy on the basis of good condition and if you're not entirely sure about something, get a second opinion or simply walk away and wait for the right car to come along. VW genuinely built enough cars to go around – and then some.

You should also consider buying a left-hand-drive car from abroad. A lot of people are apprehensive about sitting on the 'wrong' side of the car, but they really shouldn't be. All of the pedals and controls are the same as a right-hooker, the gears are in the same location, and there's nothing to catch you out. Sure, there's the odd moment here and there where you can't see around a parked vehicle to pull out, but when you drive something as charming as an old Beetle, most people tend to let you pull out and then overtake you for driving too slowly.

BODYWORK

Believe the saying that shiny isn't always best. There can be all manner of hidden horrors and bodges lurking beneath a fresh coat of paint. So, if you're looking at a car that has been 'restored', ask who carried out the work and to see some receipts. A seller with nothing to hide will be only

too keen to share this sort of information if the job has been carried out correctly and it helps sell the car, less so if they've just slapped lipstick on a pig.

A car sporting original factory paint – even when it is sunburnt and has a good smattering of surface rust – can still be a better proposition than a supposedly restored car, as you know it isn't hiding anything untoward. So where do you look? Pretty much everywhere, but there are a couple of key areas that 'go' on all Beetles.

For the first stage you don't even need to get too close. Have a general walk around the car and take it all in. Are there any bits of trim missing? Are the gaps neat and consistent on the doors, bonnet and engine lid? All of these items simply bolt on, but if they don't fit properly you need to ask yourself why. Have they been replaced with inferior reproduction panels or has the body been poorly repaired following an accident? Sagging doors are a sign of worn hinges, so if you have to lift a door up to get it to shut properly, you'll need to factor in replacing the hinge pins.

When viewing a potential purchase you should first look for trouble in the areas that will cost the most amount to put right. If these require too much work, there is usually little point bothering with everything else and it's better to cut your losses and walk away there and then.

- *Start with the metalwork around the windows.* Beetles are prone to rusting along the bottoms of the seals. Look for tell-tale bubbling in the paint and rust streaks.
- *Door and window rubbers* shrink and crack over time, even more so on imports from warmer countries. When that happens water seeps in and then collects in the lowest parts of the car, namely floorpans, which eventually rot out.
- *Cast an eye over the gutters.* These often need repair and to do so is neither an easy nor a cheap undertaking.
- *Next, take a long hard look at the front wings.* Brown streaks from behind the headlights point to rust issues and severe bubbling around the lights themselves is all too common, as is rust along the bottom edges and dents. In fact, an original-paint Beetle without a dent on at least one of the rear wings is a rare bird these days. Replacement wings are easy to come by, good quality originals a little less so, but far more serious is rust on the main bodyshell where the wings bolt to. The front and rear quarter panels are often bubbly along these areas and you also need to look for signs of corrosion along the bottoms.
- *Bumper mounts and front spare-wheel wells* are notorious rot spots, as are the sills. Not only do they add structural rigidity to a Beetle, they also carry heat from the engine to the front of the car. A car that's freezing cold in the winter but has a properly working pair of heat exchangers is often a sign of holey sills.

Sellers don't tend to like it when you pull carpet up, so open the doors and give the sills a squeeze. If they feel crunchy they're no good. You also need to check the sill closing panels underneath the car and where they meet the wheel arches. These areas are bombarded with muck and filth by the rear wheels and if it's allowed to gather, they'll rust through and the rot then creeps along the sills from the inside. Repairing this can be tricky, as to do it properly you often need to separate the body from the chassis.

Then of course there are all of your usual bits to check, such as along the bottoms of the doors and bonnet edges.

We have mentioned spare-wheel wells, but to check them from the inside you need to open the bonnet and remove the spare wheel – if there's one in there. Whilst you are there, look for bubbling on the panel where the brake fluid reservoir sits (on early cars) and for ripples that point to accident damage in the front quarters.

Doors that drop when you open them and need lifting to close properly indicate worn hinge pins.

Bubbles under the window rubbers indicate rust setting in. Holes here lead to water seeping in, destroying carpets and floorpans and anywhere else it's allowed to sit.

Cracked and damaged rubbers will allow wind noise and rain in as well as any much-needed heat out in the winter.

Wings simply bolt on, but rust on the front quarters along the wing rubber is a more complicated fix.

Rear quarters are a notorious Beetle rot spot. This one has rusted through from the inside outwards, a sure sign that water has been getting in from the inner arch and/or the sill closing plate.

Holes in the inner arch like this are the result of water and dirt being flung up by the rear wheels. This is what caused the rusty rear quarter and sill-closing panel on the featured car. The only thing to do is weld them up and repaint them.

Bumper mounts also take a hammering. In this instance they are good, which probably means they have been replaced.

Sills are notorious Beetle rot spots, although they don't usually look as bad as this on the topside. The carpet-retaining strip has been eaten away and sills in general can be pretty chewy if you give them a squeeze.

Spare wheel wells take a hammering, especially on lowered cars. This one has had a repair panel crudely welded in. It's not pretty – but at least it's solid.

Front inner wings rust as much as the rears. This one has an unsightly patch repair in one of the common areas. This car had been under-sealed from new, but the protective coating only lasts so long.

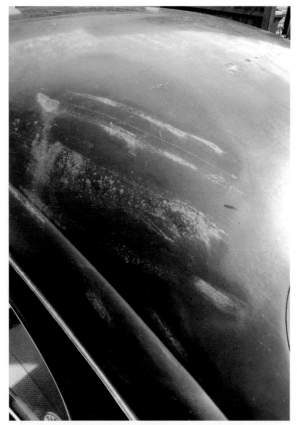

Check for rust along the bottom edges and lips of the doors, bonnet and engine lid. They are easy to remove but good quality replacements are expensive.

FLOORPAN

If you can, lift any rubber mats up that are fitted and peel the carpets back to get a good look at the chassis. Water collects in these areas and then creates its own means of escape by making rust holes. Pull the rear seat base up and have a peep under there too, especially into the corners where the heater tubes are. Again, you're looking for holes and rust caused by water damage, but you also need to check under the battery that lives under here too. Battery acid does metalwork no favours and you'll often find a repair or two under here.

Check along the gutters. Rust here is a difficult and costly repair.

Likewise the jacking points. You should never use a jack on a Beetle's jacking point nowadays, for fear of it collapsing under the weight of the car. When a lot of owners come to replace these sections they don't bother to fit a new jacking point, as they are notorious water traps.

Have a look under the car and check for rust and damage. Dented chassis spines are frustratingly common and a sign that previous owners didn't know how to jack their car up properly.

Should you need them, replacement floorpans are readily available off the shelf. You get what you pay for though and, while they are more expensive to buy, the thicker, heavier gauge replacements last longer, and are easier to fit. Frame heads also take a beating – especially on a car that has been excessively lowered – and to replace the Napoleon's Hat section is another body-off job.

Peel back carpets and mats to check for rust on the inside. Threadbare or entirely missing sill carpets are commonplace.

Cutting out rusty floorpans. Note the jacking points sticking out the side of the pan? Never trust a jack to one now…

Rusty floors are common. Surface rust can be removed with a wire wheel and repainted, but if the metal is so thin it has holed then you will need to break out the welder.

Many owners chose to remove the jacking points from new floorpans as they are horrendous water traps.

Check the area under the back seat for rot. Battery acid will merrily munch through sheet metal.

Napoleon's Hat section – so called for obvious reasons – and the frame head can rust quite badly. The body has to come off to repair them.

Original VW wiring looms will last forever as long as they are not tampered with. This one isn't the worst the author has seen.

ELECTRICS AND WIRING

Whilst you're poking around looking for rust and accident damage in the front end, you should remove the card bonnet liner and wiring cover that should be fitted. This will allow you to check on the condition of the wiring loom. There weren't a great many wires from the factory, but it's depressingly common to find a rat's nest of cables that has been built up and added to over the years by previous owners. Splicing in additional wires is often easier than tracing and fixing a wiring issue properly and things like after-market stereos and accessory spotlights can also add to the confusion when tracing faults, especially if they've been added willy-nilly using whatever colour of wiring came to hand at the time.

ENGINE AND GEARBOX

Beetles have a well-deserved reputation for reliability and longevity, but only if they've been looked after as VW intended. The first way to check this is to pull the dipstick and examine the oil. Old, black oil is a sign that it hasn't been changed at regular intervals and as air-cooled engines are actually oil-cooled that's never a good sign. The oil should be changed every 3,000 miles/once a year/ whichever comes first.

It's a common myth that all Beetles mark their spot by leaking oil, but they shouldn't. No air-cooled VW would have been allowed to leave the factory with an oil leak and yours shouldn't have one now. Sure, you can live with a few spots on the drive if you wish, but anything more serious should be properly addressed.

Most oil leaks are a cheap fix but some will require the engine to come out to reach them, especially the flywheel oil seal. You'll know this needs doing if there's a lot of oil where the engine meets the gearbox and usually a slipping clutch.

There's more in-depth information on engines later in this book, so for now, take a look at the general condition of the engine. Is it covered in oil? Are there any parts missing? How does it start and idle? Is there any smoke that points to worn rings?

1300 engine seems all right but is actually a later addition to this car, which knocks some of the value off.

A car's oil will tell you a great deal about how well it's been looked after.

One task everyone tells a would-be Beetle owner to perform is to check for end float. You do this by pulling on the bottom pulley (with the engine off of course). Any perceptible movement here means there is play in the crank and that's grounds for a new engine or a costly rebuild.

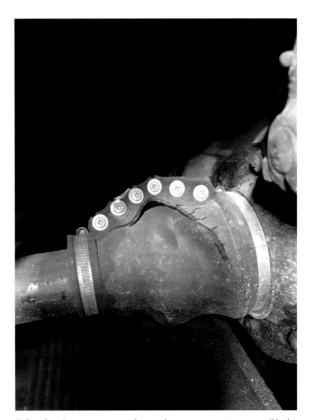

Oil on the bottom of an engine like this means there is a big leak somewhere. Flywheel oil seals can dry out if a car has been standing for a long period of time.

Split axle gaiters are commonplace and cause some pretty messy oil leaks.

Rusty exhausts and heat-exchangers are par for the course and will affect the car's heating system.

Gearboxes are pretty-much bullet proof and should give no cause for concern. Ask any Beetle owner when was the last time they changed the oil in their gearbox and they will give you a blank stare. That said, the axle gaiters tend to split, but replacing them is easy and the parts won't break the bank. However, a car that jumps out of gear means something has gone awry and the gearbox will require attention or replacing.

BRAKES AND SUSPENSION

From the factory, all early Beetles came with drum brakes front and back and king- and link-pin front suspension.

From late 1965 onwards they had ball-joint front ends but still ran drum brakes all round. The '67 1500 had discs on the front and drums on the back. All of them, bar the 1302 and 1303S, ran torsion bar suspension, which is pretty robust stuff. Front beams can rot out and damage is common on excessively lowered cars. Look for damaged adjusters and scuffed shock towers.

Narrowed beams are *de rigueur* these days, as are dropped spindles. If done properly this should cause no problems at all (well, perhaps a narrower turning circle), but on a particularly slammed car you might find the tyres rub on the inner wings or headlight bowls. Perished rubbers are depressingly common on things like ball joints and need rectifying.

Most Beetles came with torsion bars for suspension. Careful owners will have kept everything properly lubricated and replaced any worn items. Note the aftermarket adjuster that has been added to the centre of this beam.

Drum brakes work perfectly well when properly adjusted. The main issue to look for here is brake fluid leaking from a failed cylinder.

INTERIOR

There is not much to a Beetle's interior, but what there is was made to last. That said, 40 or 50 years of bums on seats will take its toll eventually. The most common materials were vinyl, or if you've bought a '50s or export model, you might find cloth seats, which are nicer but less hard wearing.

Carpets can be expensive to replace if you opt for original-style German square weave, but there are a ton of aftermarket options available at more wallet-friendly price points.

You can buy decent quality replacement rubber mats and headliners off the shelf. Fitting a new headliner is a task in itself though, so a decent original is a huge plus point, which isn't usually the case with old wool headliners. They discolour with age and split. From the mid-1960s headliners were made of white perforated vinyl and whilst they can become brittle, they tend to stay the course much better.

We should also mention radios. Beetles have a small aperture in the centre of the dash that's perfect for a period Blaupunkt. However, a great many cars have their dashboards hacked to take a large, modern head-unit. That's fine and dandy if you plan to stick with a modern set-up but incredibly disheartening if you want an original look. The only solution is to weld in a repair section and have the dash repainted.

Cloth upholstery is not so robust as later vinyl, but replacement covers are readily available for most years and models.

Early wool headliners often look like this. Horrible. Replacing them is an equally horrible task.

New carpets and mats are available off the peg and are an easy fix, although original style square weave is expensive.

Larger hole hacked for a modern head unit shows how much smaller a period radio was.

1303s have their own unique style of dashboard and later Beetles and Mexican examples have a black plastic padded dash.

EXTERIOR TRIM AND CHROME

Beetles built in the '50s and '60s have fatter trim on the sides, bonnets and running boards than cars built in the '70s. Replacements are cheap if you need some, but when it comes to bumpers you really get what you pay for. Some specialists offer repro bumpers and hubcaps with what is known as 'show chrome'. That means it's rubbish, as it was produced for a country with a 'dry climate' and will last roughly 32.5 seconds in the UK climate before it turns orange. You're better off tracking down an original item and either cleaning it up or having it re-chromed.

IDENTITY ISSUES

Always check the logbook to ensure it tallies up to the car's VIN plate. You will find a Beetle's Vehicle Identification Number riveted to the body in the spare wheel well. If it's

VIN plate can be found in the spare wheel well. Check these numbers against what is written on the log book.

The chassis number is also stamped on the frame tunnel under the back seat.

not there then you really need to ask why. Some owners remove it when restoring a car, but there's no good reason why they wouldn't put it back.

You might come across a car that's had a bodyshell from one year mounted on a replacement chassis from another. This would have been done if a car was especially rotten or, for example, if the owner wanted to run a later IRS chassis under an earlier-style body.

You will find a number stamped on the chassis spine under the rear seat that should tie up with the one on the VIN plate. If it doesn't tally up, you will know it's not a matching numbers car. It isn't the end of the world if it does not match what's on the logbook, but it is important to a lot of buyers who want to see a matching numbers car. A car that doesn't have matching numbers will be worth less and you should take this into consideration before handing over any money.

KNOW WHEN TO WALK AWAY

Being able to say 'thanks, but no thanks' and pass on a car that isn't right for you is something that will stand any wannabe Beetle owner in good stead. There are so many cars out there that you can afford to be picky and walk away from one that doesn't tick all of your boxes.

For the purposes of writing this book, the black '58 that appears throughout was perfect. It needed the lot – bodywork, engine, suspension, brakes, wheels and interior – so we would be able to document all of the work along the way.

However, if the author was looking to buy a Beetle simply for himself, he would most likely have walked away from this one. Most likely? Well, despite it needing so much work it is a really desirable model. Being a '58 it has loads of neat features, such as the ice-pick door handles, semaphore indicators, snowflake taillights and late Oval steering wheel.

Being a factory black car also adds to the appeal and none of the above grows on trees, so when you're buying an old car, there is an element of having to buy what's out there.

This car ticked all the 'want' boxes, but the author would have passed on it due to the amount of work it needed to make it right. Producing this book and the fact that it fell into the author's lap when it was offered in part-exchange against a more expensive car, is the reason you're looking at it now.

Despite the author going into this project with his eyes open, he still managed to underestimate the amount of time, effort and money it took to get it to a driveable state. As with any old car, he uncovered additional work he hadn't planned for along the way, work and family commitments impacted on his time and there were periods where he simply lacked the motivation to be out in the garage working on the car. If that can happen to the author, it can happen to anyone. But, as the old saying goes, the juice was worth the squeeze and the author has come out of the end of the tunnel with a really fabulous little car and it's something he can proudly say he did himself.

Taken in part exchange, we knew the featured project car needed work but underestimated exactly how much.

4

Tools: What You Need to Fix Your Bug's Bugs

Old VWs need TLC. Even fully restored ones will need more looking after than your modern, daily driver and you should see the need to replace the oil and check the tappets from time-to-time as part of their charm, rather than an inconvenience. See routine maintenance as an opportunity to bond with your car and understand its inner workings. Do that and you'll learn how to fix it if and when it does go wrong.

An air-cooled VW isn't like a modern car and so you shouldn't expect to treat it as such. The likes of VW, Audi

TOP: *You don't need a lot of fancy tools to work on a Beetle, but it does make life easier if you have good-quality equipment and multiples of certain sizes. A vintage Hazet toolbox to store them is an extravagance, but if they were good enough for VW mechanics to use in the dealerships, they are good enough for someone keeping the VW alive today.*

and every other car manufacturer today doesn't want you or I spannering on their latest wares. If a warning light pings up on the dashboard of a modern car and you refer to the manual, the only advice you'll get now is to return the car to the dealership.

However, old VWs positively encourage you to get your hands dirty, be it replacing worn out components or simply sticking to the specified servicing intervals. If you want your VW to look after you, you will need to look after it in return. All of which means you'll need to arm yourself with the correct tools.

FINDING WHAT YOU NEED

Fortunately, you don't need much to keep an air-cooled VW in tip-top condition and what you *do* need you can amass over a period of time. Don't be fooled into thinking you need to rush out and buy all of this in one hit, or that you need to buy well-known (expensive) brands. Buying second hand at swap meets and car boot sales is a great way to build-up a collection of tools on the cheap. Find something in a box of junk at a boot sale and the likelihood is the seller will have little or no interest in it, so you can buy it for next

to nothing. This applies especially to metric tools, as there is a tendency for the people selling this sort of stuff to place little value on anything without an imperial measurement. Their ignorance can be your gain.

So, what do you need to mend a poorly Beetle? Allow us to elaborate.

METRIC NOT IMPERIAL

Okay, first things first – sockets and spanners. The vast majority of VWs were made in Germany, so all of the fastenings will be in metric sizes. This makes life easier as you won't have to think in fractions of an inch when digging around for the right tool. In fact, the most commonly used sizes on an air-cooled VW are 10, 13, 15, 17 and 19mm, so it helps to have multiples of these.

A set like this is great, as it means you have pretty much everything to hand when you need it.

Manual

Knowledge is power and this book is a guide to rather than a detailed manual that covers everything in minute detail, so the more books and manuals you have covering your specific model and year of car, the better. Charity shops, car boot sales and the internet are great places to pick these up cheaply.

Socket set

You don't have to buy everything in one big hit. A cheap socket set will come with everything you need to do most simple tasks, but you should really try to buy the best you can afford. Poor quality tools can round off nuts and bolts and lead to skimmed knuckles. The Halfords Professional range strikes a good balance between price and quality and comes with a life-time guarantee, so if something breaks, they'll replace it free of charge. Long-reach sockets will come in handy and a selection of different length extensions will be required. Most fittings you encounter will be between 10 and 19mm, but you'll need a 36mm socket for removing a rear hub or flywheel nut.

John Muir's Step by Step Procedures for the Compleat Idiot *is a legendary read in VW circles. It's funny, informative and a must-have for any Beetle owner.*

Sockets are metric sizes, but the interface on the ratchet that attaches to the socket come in ¼ inch, ⅜ or ½ inch sizes. You will use the ⅜ drive for most jobs requiring a 10–19mm socket.

Spanners

You will be using these a lot, so again, try to buy the best ones you can afford, or keep your eyes peeled for a decent quality old set online or at a show. You'll need the same sizes as we've mentioned in the section on sockets, but you'll need multiples of all the common sizes, in both open and ring ends.

Cranked and ratchet spanners are useful for working in confined spaces, but a ratchet spanner won't stand up to the sort of abuse a good-quality ring spanner can absorb.

Some screwdrivers have a shaped handle that allows you to slip a spanner over them to apply additional torque.

Screwdrivers

A basic set of Pozi-drive and flat-head drivers are a must, as they'll be able to perform most tasks on a Beetle. You'll also need to buy a couple of stubby-handled drivers for areas with limited access. Resist the temptation to use a screwdriver as a pry bar or chisel, as that will damage the driver's ends and mangle any fittings or fastenings you're attempting to budge.

Pliers and cutters

Pliers come in a variety of styles in order to carry out specific tasks. Having a good selection of sizes and lengths means you'll be able to get to grips on most jobs. Regular and long-nose pliers are a good starting point, as are a basic pair of wire cutters/strippers.

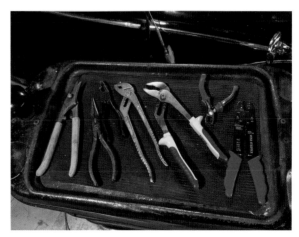

Pliers are essential for getting a firm grip on anything that won't budge or you need to apply heat to.

Perfect for rounding off heads and ruining everything they touch, but when you really need to hold something in place or it just needs to come off so you can replace it, one of these can do the trick.

Some emergency breakdown services don't even carry feeler gauges anymore, so make sure you have some in your car at all times. They are an absolute must for any classic car owner.

Mole grips and adjustable spanners

Controversial, as you really should use the correct size socket on a fastening where possible, but everyone has a selection of these in their war chest, just in case.

Circlip pliers

Circlips can be a pig to remove even when you have the right tools to hand, so pick a pair of these up when you can. They don't cost much, and you'll be glad you invested in a pair when you do come to need them.

Feeler gauges

These are essential tools for carrying out any routine service work. You'll need them to set the points, valves and spark-plug gaps to ensure your engine runs properly.

Breaker bar and torque wrench

These might be roughly the same size, but don't use one where you should be using the other. A breaker bar can

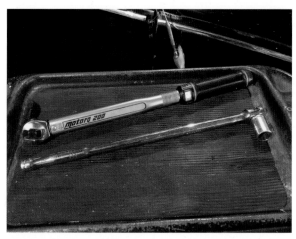

Breaker bars are perfect for when you need to apply a bit of extra muscle and a torque wrench tells you when to take things easy. Always slacken off the adjuster when it's not in use.

help loosen any stubborn nuts and bolts, whereas the torque wrench is essential for tightening any components that require precise tolerances. Overtightening certain fastenings, such as cylinder heads and sump nuts, can pull them out of the case. Sometimes less is more, so always adhere to the torque settings as laid out in your workshop manual.

Inspection light

Even if you're working outdoors, you'll need one of these to be able to peer into all the dark nooks and crannies of a Beetle. It helps to have more than one if they're the rechargeable type, because they have an annoying tendency to run out of juice right when you need them.

Protective gear

Health and safety is a boring subject, but you can do yourself an awful lot of damage working on old cars. Eye, hand, ear and breathing protection is a must, as you really don't want metal shards in your peepers and an angle grinder makes horrifyingly short work of skin.

Circlip pliers come with a variety of jaw attachments. A simple set like this will suffice for pretty much any job on a Beetle.

This inspection light has a magnetic base, which helps with positioning it and keeping both hands free to work.

Gloves for keeping your hands clean are one thing, but you will need something a little more heavy-duty if you want to avoid burning your skin on hot metal or cutting yourself on jagged edges.

Angle grinder

Even if you're not cutting out rot and restoring metalwork, an angle grinder will come in handy for removing stubborn fastenings and worn-out components in a hurry. Go easy with them: they're not known as 'death wheels' for nothing, you know.

Belt sander

A finger sander is ideal for getting into tight spots and delicate trim work. It's also super useful for grinding down big, fat welds if you're a novice welder.

Always wear the appropriate safety gear and keep all of the guards in place when using a grinder.

Ensure you have plenty of belts to hand when working with a sander, as you can go through them pretty sharpish.

Dremel

A Dremel does pretty much the same thing as an angle grinder, but on a much smaller scale. You might not use it a lot, but it's handy to have around all the same.

Perfect for delicate cutting and making tiny modifications.

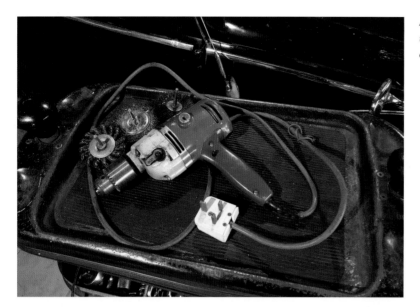

A modern cordless drill is fine and dandy, but this old beast can be run for ages without overheating and it never runs out of power.

Drill

You'll need one of these for removing spot welds in panels or drilling out an old fastening or broken bolt. A wire wheel (aka cheek poker) on the end is ideal for removing dirt and rust from old components.

Extension leads

An obvious one if you're using power tools, because no matter where you're working, or how you've parked your car, when you're plugged in you're never in the right spot. An extension cable takes care of that and helps you charge up/run multiple items at the same time.

Measuring tools

A lot of people say you need to measure twice and cut once, but it's best to measure as many times as you need to before you commit to chopping into anything. A metal rule and tape measure are the minimum requirements for making anything in the garage.

Accurate measurement is essential for many of the jobs your Beetle will create for you.

With great power comes a great extension lead. Sorry, but you will need one of these.

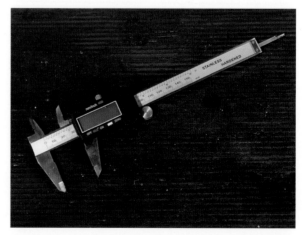

Vernier gauges are useful for accurate measurements and one like this will only set you back a couple of pounds.

A Sharpie works just as well as a graphite pencil, but this is more old school and takes much longer to run out.

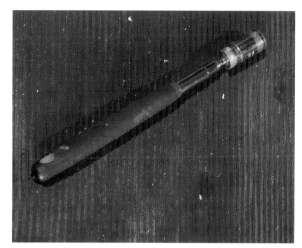

This magnet has an LED light on the end, which makes it a little easier to spot any fastenings that have gone missing.

Pencils, scribes and punches

Again, not exactly necessary if you're not making anything, but super useful when you are. As is a role of masking tape. The graphite pencil will leave its mark anywhere and the nail punch is a must-have if you're drilling into metalwork and don't want the drill bit to slip.

Telescopic/magnetic pick-up

You will drop nuts, bolts and screws into spaces your fingers simply can't reach, so one of these in your toolbox can really get you out of trouble. You never want to leave metal fastenings behind fanbelts or anywhere they can fall in or fire off and cause harm.

Trim removal tools

These are made of plastic and cost peanuts to buy. They'll stop you from scratching paintwork and digging into delicate pieces of aluminium trim.

A few pounds spent on these can reduce the pain and expense of replacing damaged trim.

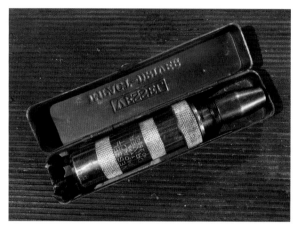

This impact screwdriver cost just £3 from a car boot sale. Money well spent.

Impact screwdriver

We're getting into the realms of specialist tools here, but one of these will come in super-handy for loosening seized or stubborn screws, for example Beetle door hinges. Simply place it on the offending screw head and give it a wallop with a hammer. That usually does the trick and shouldn't damage the screw head either.

Specialist tools

Everything in this chapter was bought at one time or another to carry out a specific task at hand. Items like ball-joint splitters, the flywheel locking tool, clutch alignment tool, brake hose clamps, brake adjusting tool, spark plug spanner, trailing arm removal tool, and electrical circuit tester/probe light were simply bought when the need arose.

Miscellaneous tools

Every now and then you'll find something like a CV joint or torsion bar grub screw that requires an Allen key to remove it, so these are a handy addition to your toolbox. As are a decent mallet, soldering iron and clamps.

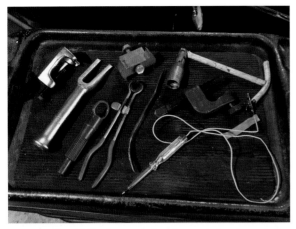

More specialist tools like these can be bought as and when the need arises, or simply borrowed from a friend if they have them.

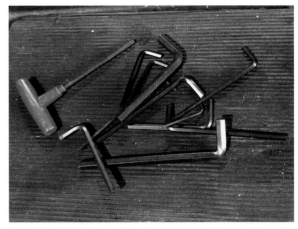

Research any jobs before starting; that way you won't find yourself stuck due to lacking the right tool.

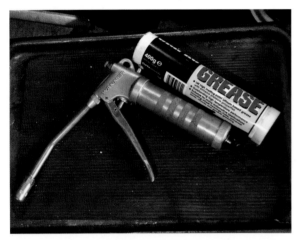

It might be older than God's dog, but this grease gun still does the trick and costs less than a pint of beer to buy.

Grease gun

One of these is essential for routine maintenance work on a Beetle. There are a number of front suspension points on a Bug that require regular greasing and once you've bought one for yourself, you'll be able to carry out the work whenever suits you.

Jacks/axle stands

You will need to raise your car off the ground from time-to-time to work on items such as the brakes and suspension, so you will need a good quality jack that can cope with the load. You want something with a minimum 2-ton weight rating. The same goes for the axle stands, which you should always place underneath a car, as you should never rely solely on a jack. Always work on firm ground so nothing sinks or moves in any way. You can buy wheel chocks or use blocks of wood or bricks to prevent a car from rolling.

Ramps are great, but are only really for stock cars. Most modified VWs are too low to get up them. These have a handy feature in that they have bottle jacks to raise the platforms even higher once the car is sitting on them.

A low-lift jack is required for getting under a lowered car, but you might still have to drive your car onto blocks first to get a jack under it.

Air compressor

Being able to check tyre pressures at home is nice, but more importantly you can run all manner of air tools from a compressor. Things like windy guns, air chisels and paint guns mean you can carry out a lot of the more specialist jobs yourself, saving you money and increasing your skill set.

Welder

One of these will come in handy, even if you're not going to be tackling major metalwork repairs yourself. You can make quick or temporary repairs on things like exhausts and the author has even used this one to weld a metal bar

You can still accomplish a surprising amount with a small hobby compressor like this, but you need to check they have enough power to run certain tools.

A sturdy workbench and enough space to take things apart, clean, restore, paint and store them is a must have if you are planning to work on any classic car.

Bench vice

Very handy for holding things you might need to cut, drill or heat up; a bench vice like this is a firm pair of hands when you need them. It might not be up to the task of holding larger items, but this little one has coped with everything the author has thrown at it so far, hence he has never felt the need to replace it with a larger one.

This is just a cheap, gasless welder. For more serious welding you will need to invest in one more suited to the task.

onto a broken beam bolt. The combination of heat and extra leverage was enough to get the offending bolt out of the frame head.

Workspace

Think about your workspace. Is it nearby? If you have to drive miles to work on your car, it's not like you can just nip out and spend twenty minutes here and there. You'll have to commit blocks of time to be able to work on it. That's not easy when you have a job and family commitments, which are two of the main reasons a lot of restorations go unfinished.

Also, in terms of location, what are the neighbours like? Are they going to be okay with you crashing around and making noise with air tools into the wee small hours? This is something that is definitely worth considering.

As is security and insurance. You should ensure your garage/workshop is as secure as possible and that your vehicle is insured, because if any of it goes missing as a result of unwanted visitors you'll be out of pocket to say the least. Even if your car is an unregistered project you can have it insured on the chassis number and with an agreed value with most decent insurance companies.

Don't laugh. This has still proven super useful and was bought for peanuts at a car boot sale.

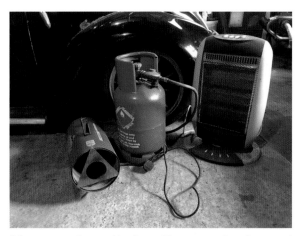

Take care not to place anything flammable on or around your heaters and regularly check the condition of any gas fittings or hoses.

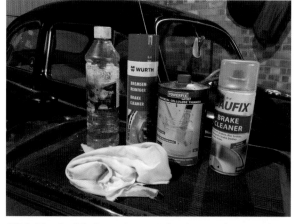

Old clothing should be kept as it comes in handy as rags for wiping down car parts, work surfaces, tools and even yourself.

Heat

Few things suck away at your motivation more than working in a cold garage. Half an hour of standing or lying on a cold concrete floor or handling stone-cold tools is enough for anyone. A gas heater can be used to rapidly bring a garage up to temperature and the electric heater helps maintain it at a comfortable level.

Lubricants

Rusted and seized fittings can be persuaded to come off by applying a little 'get out of there' juice, be it WD40 or similar. Once a stubborn fastener has been removed you can ensure its replacement doesn't take any inspiration from its predecessor by applying some copper grease.

Cleaning solutions

You'll go through a lot of cleaning products, be they brake cleaner, paint thinners or whatever. Oily components will need to be thoroughly cleaned before you can repaint them; tools should be wiped down before you put them

away to avoid transferring dirt to the next job you use them on; and even cleaning yourself after a hard day in the garage.

A GOOD BREW

Never underestimate the power of a good cup of tea. Taking a break from a job that's been busting your chops for the last hour always helps. It gives you space to calm down and allows you to think up a new plan of attack. Knowing when to walk away can seriously reduce the number of flung spanners and fruity language emanating from the garage.

England expects every man (and woman) to do their duty and your better half will thank for only using old mugs in the garage. You have been warned.

Metal-on-metal and years of being exposed to the elements can make removing stubborn bolts are real chore. Penetrating oil or, failing that, heat can help break them free.

5

Service and Maintenance

Beetles and air-cooled VWs in general have a well-deserved reputation for reliability. And, whilst this is true, they were/ are more reliable than most of their contemporaries, it's a bit of a double-edged sword. You see, a lot of people take this reputation for granted and don't look after them as they should, assuming they'll soldier on forever because they're so reliable…. This blinkered approach is a sure-fire way to ruin any car and, if you do the same, you'll soon find yourself stranded on the side of the road, cursing the day you ever bought the thing.

The way to avoid breakdowns and running issues is simple. Treat your car to the TLC it deserves, address any faults and issues as soon as they become apparent and everything should be dandy.

When it was new, VW recommended servicing your Beetle once a year or every 3,000 miles, whichever came first. So that's what the author has always done himself and recommends to you now.

When you choose to service your car is entirely up to you, but as most owners now put their cars away over the winter, it is a good idea to service yours in the spring so it's ready for the year ahead.

Servicing your Bug is not only essential to ensure reliable motoring, it's the perfect opportunity to check over the entire car in detail to ensure that nothing has gone south during the cold months spent sitting in the garage.

TOP: *Carrying out your own service work will teach you how your car works and how to fix it if and when it breaks.*

USEFUL TIP

It's one of the strange quirks of classic cars, but things like rubber boots on suspension components can split for no reason whatsoever, electrical terminals can corrode, the surface on your points can rust and brake cylinders can leak. In fact, there are all manner of things an old car can and will do if it's left to its own devices, so you're much better off using or at least starting your car on a regular basis rather than allowing it to sit idle.

WEEKLY CHECKS

Whilst this will be an alien concept to drivers of modern cars, as a Beetle owner you should get used to carrying out weekly, if not daily, checks on your machine. Every classic car owner on the planet drives with one ear constantly tuned to their vehicle. Any sudden bang, clonk, rumble or whine will immediately become their sole focus of attention, even if their passenger says they can't hear a thing.

As a caring Beetle owner, you should regularly check the oil on the dipstick and every time before taking it on a longer journey.

Fire is a major cause for concern on any air-cooled VW. When fuel lines perish, or an uncaring owner omits to fit a clamp, petrol drips onto hot engine components and leads to disaster. Therefore, regularly check the condition of your fuel lines and change them if necessary.

Air-cooled VWs rely on their cooling fan to keep them at a comfortable operating temperature. Check the tension and condition of the fanbelt to ensure it's working as it should and is not about to self-destruct. Driving without a fanbelt will cook your engine in a matter of minutes.

Set aside a day once a year and your VW will thank you for it. Working on solid ground – ideally indoors – really helps, too.

You should also cast an eye over and top-up fluid levels in your washer bottle and brake fluid reservoir. If the latter needs topping up it means there's a leak somewhere and something is amiss with your brakes. Likewise, tyre pressures: they should be correctly inflated to ensure even tyre wear and safe handling.

YEARLY/3,000–MILE CHECKS

All of these jobs come under the heading of a yearly service and consist of the following: replacing the oil and filter; changing the points and condenser; checking/replacing the rotor arm and spark plugs; checking/adjusting the valve clearances; checking/adjusting brakes; checking/adjusting wheel bearings; checking/topping-up gearbox oil; greasing the front axle; and cleaning/topping-up the air filter.

We'll now look at each of these tasks in more detail.

SAFETY FIRST

Some of these jobs have to be carried out underneath the car. This means you'll need to raise it up. Whenever you raise your car off the ground, you'll need to ensure that it is safely supported. Never rely solely on a jack, always use good quality axle stands and only ever on solid, level ground.

At the very least, you should check the oil every week and cast an eye over the engine bay.

Axle stands are an absolute must; never rely solely on a jack to support your Beetle whilst it's in the air.

Draining the engine oil

An air-cooled flat-four engine requires oil to lubricate and cool its internals. If you don't change it at least every 3,000 miles or fail to top it up if the level drops, your engine won't be long for this world.

Place a suitable container underneath to catch the oil and remove the sump plate to drain it from the engine. Later cars and aftermarket parts have a 21mm (0.8in) drain plug in the middle of the sump plate, which makes this a slightly cleaner job.

If you're working with an early sump plate, you won't have a drain plug so will have to remove the six small acorn nuts around the circumference of the plate to drain the oil. Rather than slackening them all off in one go, remove a few from one side first. That way, the plate will drop down at an angle and the oil will pour to one side. Warm oil will drain faster than cold, so it helps if you've run the car for a few minutes before you do this. You don't want it too hot and it's best to avoid touching hot metal components, such as the exhaust.

Old engine oil is carcinogenic, so wear gloves and dispose of it properly. Your local tip should have a collection point you can pour it into.

Oil strainer

Whilst the oil is draining, take the time to clean up the oil strainer. Replacements are cheap and plentiful and if you pay a little extra for your oil change kit, one will be included in the price. However, the only time the author ever tried to install a new one, the gauze filter wouldn't fit over the oil

If you haven't got any engine degreaser you can use brake/carb cleaner or old petrol to clean the oil strainer.

This is an early sump plate without the central drain plug. Go easy with those nuts to avoid pulling the studs from the case.

pickup tube without a little fettling (he used an old socket and hammer to enlarge the opening).

An original VW part is always better than a pattern replacement, so it is usually enough to give them a thorough clean with rags and brake cleaner to remove the sludge, so there's no reason why you can't do that as well.

These are the only oil filters stock Beetles come with (although you can install an accessory filter), so ensure it's clean before it goes back in.

Sump gaskets

The rest of your oil change kit will consist of two paper gaskets and soft copper washers for the sump nuts. If it's for a later sump, there will also be a copper crush washer for the central drain plug.

You can't re-use the old gaskets and the order for fitting the new ones goes as follows. The first of the paper gaskets mates to the engine case; the oil strainer goes on next; followed by the other gasket and finally the metal sump plate.

Before fitting, you need to ensure all of the mating surfaces are clean of dirt and any residue of old gasket. A sharp Stanley knife blade does the job. Some owners use a little sealant to ensure there are no leaks, but that shouldn't be necessary unless your strainer is all beaten out of shape.

A tiny smear of fresh grease helps hold the gasket in place whilst you get everything lined up and fitted, but you need to go carefully with the small sump nuts. Muscle does more harm than good here and if you over-tighten them you run the risk of pulling the studs from the case.

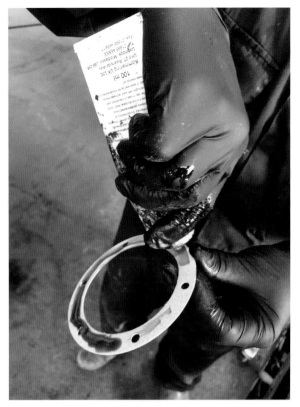

You can use a smear of gasket sealant if you wish, but it means more clean-up work when you come to do it again next time.

Use a funnel to fill the oil, or else it will go everywhere. An old AdBlue container (cleaned out) is the perfect oil can/filler.

Sump plate

Use a torque wrench and tighten the sump nuts up to 5ft/lb, which isn't very much at all. Cheaper torque wrenches aren't especially accurate at such low settings, so most owners tend to do this by feel, which is something you'll develop with experience.

Go easy on those sump nuts. They just need to be snug.

Engine oil

A 1600cc Beetle engine should hold 2.5 litres of oil. Don't pour it all in at once but keep adding a little at a time and regularly check the dipstick to ensure you don't over fill it.

Many people swear by 30 weight oil, but a modern 20W50 will be fine. Basically, you need something with a good amount of minerals in it to really coat the internals. Lots of brands are available, but the author tends to favour Morris Golden Film SAE 30, which he picks up at VW shows, or Halfords Classic Motor Oil (the green and cream metal can) when he needs some in a hurry.

Oil bath/air filter

There is another part of the engine that requires an oil change – the oil bath air filter that sits on top of the carburettor. These are often changed for aftermarket filters with paper elements, but from the factory your engine would have an oil bath filter. Nobody ever changes the oil in these; well, not unless they've stored it badly and the oil has poured out, but the oil is a key ingredient for the air filter. Dirt and dusty air is drawn across it and sticks in the oil. Little wonder that it should require changing. Drain the old oil and fill to the red line with fresh oil. The same stuff you've used in the engine is fine.

Distributor cap

Pop the dizzy cap off and examine it for cracks and other signs of damage. Take a peep at the electrodes and give

Clean out and fill the oil bath filter to the line with fresh engine oil.

An early style, genuine VW rotor. Yours will look something like this and can only go on one way.

Most people use the same cap for years, which is fine – but it's good to carry a spare.

A rare sight: original VW points and condenser (the little canister on the side of the distributor with the green wire running to the coil).

Points

There's no point reusing points. They're a cheap consumable, so take the old set off and stick them in your 'just in case' stash. They come in a variety of styles so ensure you have the correct replacements – this is why we recommend you keep hold of the old set; you never know if or when they'll come in handy. Points don't come with the retaining screw, so you'll have to re-use the one you removed. Try not to drop it.

Setting the points gap

Loosely screw the new points into place and turn the bottom pulley until the points open on the cam. Set the contact-breaker gap to 0.4mm (0.016-in) using a feeler gauge and tighten the fixing screw. Use the feeler gauge to ensure the gap didn't move when you tightened the retaining screw. You want it so the gauge slightly drags as you slide it through the gap. You'll develop a feel for this.

Always fit a new condenser. Again, they come in a variety of flavours, with different mountings and either a square or round terminal that pushes into the distributor base.

Drop a tiny amount of oil into the recess on top of the distributor shaft to lubricate it and pop the cap back on. Job done.

them a clean with a wire brush if you see any signs of corrosion. Pull off the rotor arm and place it to one side for later, or in your stash of spare parts, and fit a replacement. Caps and rotors are cheap to replace, but most Beetle owners use the same ones for years, especially if they have a more attractive, old-style distributor cap.

Rotor

These last until they need replacing. Sounds silly, but again, most people just keep reusing the same one that's been on the car since who knows when. Fitting a new one is fine and dandy, but there's no point in replacing a genuine VW part with an inferior replacement just because you have one.

Removing the distributor and placing it in a vice can make this job a little easier. Just make a note or scribe a mark to show where it lined up before you do.

This job scares a lot of new VW owners but is easy once you know how and is essential for a smooth-running, reliable and long-lived engine.

Spark plugs

Plugs should be examined, cleaned or replaced every 8,050–16,100km (5,000–10,000 miles), but as they come with a lot of service kits, it would be good practice to change them whenever you service your engine. They can be a little fiddly to change, especially if your engine is fitted with twin carbs. Getting them out is the easy part, especially if you have the right tool to get to them; the harder part is fitting new ones without cross-threading them. Check the gaps before fitting them as it should be 0.7mm (0.028in) on engines fitted with regular coils. You don't want to over-tighten them – just half a turn past hand-tight is plenty. If your plug leads look or feel like they are past their prime, take the opportunity to replace these as well.

You will need to use the feeler gauge to check the gap; don't just assume they will be correct right out of the box.

Valve clearances

An engine needs to be stone cold to set these, so either tackle them first or you'll have to come back to them the day after you've run the car to drop the oil.

Pop the rocker covers off and have a rag handy to catch any oil that trickles out. Remove the dizzy cap and locate the notch in the rim of the distributor body. There will also be a notch on the bottom (crankshaft) pulley (or three), which are your top dead centre (TDC) timing marks. Use a 30mm spanner on the bottom pulley to turn the engine until the rotor arm is pointing at the notch on the dizzy and the TDC line on the pulley is lined up with centre line of the crank case halves. That's number one cylinder firing at TDC. Numbers one and two cylinders are on the right as you look at the engine from behind, three and four on the left. Tappet gaps should be 0.15mm (0.006-inch) and the feeler blade should just slide between the tappet screw and valve with a hint of resistance. To adjust, slacken the lock nut and screw in or out and then retighten the nut. Check with the gauge to ensure the gap is still correct and then turn the pulley 180 degrees anticlockwise opposite the TDC mark. The engine is now firing on number two cylinder. Check and adjust the tappet as necessary. Rotating it another 180 degrees has the engine firing on number three cylinder and another 180 degrees has it firing on number four. It's easy when you know how. Always fit new rocker cover gaskets or you'll end up with leaks.

Gearbox oil

This is something no one ever bothers to check, but you really should. Your car needs to be level in order to do this and you will have to climb underneath to check the fluid level, so be extra careful. Once you've shuffled underneath, you'll need to locate the filler/inspection plug on the nearside of the case. Remove it and poke your finger inside to see if you can feel any oil. The gearbox has the right amount of oil inside when it is level with the brim of the case. Any lower and you need to add some more, how much depends on how much is in there.

You will need a squeezy bottle with a long flexible spout to fill the gearbox. To change the oil in the box you simply

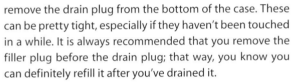

In this shot you can clearly see the drain plug on the left and the clutch lever to the right.

You will need a torch to see inside the drum and find the star adjusters.

remove the drain plug from the bottom of the case. These can be pretty tight, especially if they haven't been touched in a while. It is always recommended that you remove the filler plug before the drain plug; that way, you know you can definitely refill it after you've drained it.

Whilst you're under there take the opportunity to lubricate the clutch cable and check for play in the foot pedal. It should be 10–25mm (0.4–1in). Wind the wingnut in or out to adjust as necessary.

Brakes

Carry out a visual inspection of the copper brake lines and rubber flexi-hoses. You're looking for bulges, splits or corroded lines. Spot anything of this sort and you need to replace them immediately. Brake fluid should be changed every two years and topped up if needs be in between.

Early Beetles were equipped with drums all round and later ones have discs on the front and drums on the rear. With the car raised off the ground and supported by axle stands, the wheels can be spun by hand. You want a hint of drag on drum brakes. VW recommends adjusting every 9,650km (6,000 miles) and to do this you need to poke your brake adjusting tool (although most people just use a screwdriver) through the adjuster hole in the drum and turn the star adjuster until the desired result is achieved.

The adjuster hole is in the front of the drum on early cars and in the backing plate, at the rear of the drum on later cars. Press the brake pedal to centre the shoe and check again. For disc brakes, remove the wheel and check the pads for wear. Once you've adjusted the drums you can adjust the handbrake. There are adjusters on either side of

the handbrake lever, inside the rubber boot if there's one fitted, slacken off the lock nut and then adjust as necessary. A handbrake should pull up no more than five clicks.

Grease front axle

Whilst the car is up in the air, take the opportunity to lubricate the front suspension. There are five points that require lubing every 8,050km (5,000 miles). These are the steering idler pin in the centre of the beam and the four trailing arm bushes at the ends of each torsion bar. Early VWs also have kingpins with grease nipples that require lubing too.

Clean any dirt and grime off the nipples with a cloth and use a grease gun filled with a good general purpose or

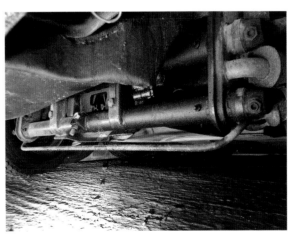

In this picture you can see the grease nipples on the ends of the axle tubes. Link pins also require lubricating on early cars.

graphite type grease. Pump until fresh grease oozes out of the seals and then wipe off the excess.

Fanbelt

If the fanbelt grenades on you, the engine will cook itself in next to no time. Check the belt for fraying, cracks or splits and fit a new one if needs be. They also need the right amount of tension to operate correctly. Too slack and they won't charge, too tight and they will destroy the bearings in the generator/alternator. You want about 13mm (1/2in) deflection. To adjust the tension, you simply add or remove the shims from behind the top pulley accordingly.

Timing

Correct engine timing is essential to achieve smooth running, maximum performance and decent fuel economy. That said, most people don't own an engine timer. The reason being, you can get around buying one if you have a friend who owns one, or if you are happy to pay for a VW specialist to set your engine's timing.

The author has always made do with a £5 circuit tester, which is all you need to statically time an air-cooled flat four. In order to do this, you first need to ensure the engine is firing on cylinder number one and is at top dead centre (TDC). The notches on the bottom pulley will tell you when that's been achieved.

VW fitted a number of different pulleys over the years; aftermarket versions often have timing markings across the full face of the pulley, which is very handy, but a stock VW pulley will have just one, two or three markings on it.

Most VW engines are timed at 7.5 degrees before TDC. If your pulley has two marks you want to use the mark on the left, if your pulley has three marks it's the one in the middle and if it only has one mark just use that one to get it to TDC.

Pop the dizzy cap off and turn the engine until the rotor arm is pointing towards the notch on the distributor body (number one cylinder) and the 7.5 before TDC mark on the pulley is at 12 o'clock/in-line with the seam in the engine case.

Loosen the 10mm retaining nut on the distributor clamp so you can turn the dizzy by hand and then clip the end of your circuit tester to the negative side of the coil – this is the side the distributor wire goes to. Ground the end of the circuit tester against a suitable part of the engine and then turn the ignition on. Rotate the distributor clockwise until the light goes out and then turn it back anti-clockwise until the light first comes on. Tighten the 10mm nut on the clamp, pop the dizzy cap back on and you should have a sweetly running engine.

If the engine feels sluggish you may want to time it closer to 10 degrees before TDC for more advance (the mark on the right, if you have two marks on your pulley). Some engines with an 009 distributor are happier nearer to 9 degrees initial advance. Experiment until you find the sweet spot. This is when a timing gun proves its worth.

A crucial component. If this is too tight it can destroy generator bearings; too loose and it won't charge the electrical system or cool the engine properly.

If you have a degree pulley and timing light, you can set the time to 28 degrees total advance – revving the engine to full distributor advance.

GENERAL BITS AND BOBS

A caring owner will also cast an eye over things like the windscreen wipers and tyres. Both wear over time and reduced visibility plus worn or incorrectly inflated tyres are dangerous.

You should take a few minutes to lubricate the door locks, hinges and handles to ensure nothing sticks and to increase longevity.

A few minutes on the little jobs can save a lot of money and hassle in the long run.

Keeping on top of the little jobs can help fend off the need for larger repairs and bigger bills later.

Engine and Related Systems

6.1 Identifying and buying

If you have never worked on an air-cooled engine before they can come across as strange little things, simply because they don't look like a regular car engine. However, once you've got your head around them, you will realize that they are incredibly simple things and a marvellous example of German engineering.

The engine itself is entirely hidden away from sight, so what you actually see when you open the engine lid are all the ancillaries – the generator/alternator, carburettor,

TOP: *If you need a replacement engine for any reason, there are a number of options available, both new and secondhand.*

distributor, coil – and that's about it. However, these are all the essential bits you need to look after the engine, so working on an air-cooled engine is easy once you know where everything should be.

There are two things you will have to get used to hearing once you've bought a Beetle. The first is that the engine is only held in by four bolts. This is, in fact, true – although there are a few other bits and bobs you have to remove before you can pop an engine out. The second thing is that a Porsche engine bolts straight in. This is rubbish. Well, assuming the person saying that is talking about a six-cylinder 911 engine, at least.

In truth, you can fit a six-cylinder Porsche engine in a Beetle, but only after a monstrous amount of work has gone into the chassis, added extra strengthening and a lot of additional room has been made for it. Simply put, a Porsche flat six is just too large and far too heavy for a VW Beetle, so feel free to laugh in the face of the next person you hear spouting this old chestnut.

A four-cylinder Porsche engine from a 356, 912 or 914 *will* fit in the blunt end of a Beetle, but even they will require a bit of work to things like tinware, exhausts, clutches and so on. They are also pretty expensive, as anything with a Porsche part number tends to be, so the chances of you coming across a Beetle equipped with a bona fide Porsche engine in the wild are pretty small.

It is common to find a Beetle fitted with a later or larger capacity engine than the one it left the factory with. This can be a good or bad thing, depending on your point of view. For the sake of originality and value, especially with an early car, factory original is king. A matching numbers car (one that retains both its original engine and gearbox) is always going to command more money at sale, but a later, larger capacity engine is going to improve the driving experience and make maintenance a little easier/cheaper.

There are all manner of reasons why a Beetle might have lost its original factory-fitted engine, but the common ones are because it suffered a catastrophic failure of some kind, a previous owner simply wanted to upgrade the car and fit something with a little more power, or they've been taken out of a project car and fitted in some other VW instead. None of which is the end of the world. Replacement units are available to buy off the shelf as complete, ready-to-go, turnkey engines.

You can opt for what the car originally came with or go for something with a bit more poke. It all just depends on what you want and how much you're willing to spend.

For those keeping tabs on the purse strings, it's ridiculously easy to buy a secondhand replacement that's been removed from another vehicle. Look online or in the back of any of the specialist VW magazines and you'll see that they are cheap enough. At the time of writing this book, a complete but ropey-looking Beetle engine could be picked up for as little as £500, which is pretty much the price they have always been, but the cheaper an engine is, the more work it will undoubtedly need. The trick is to know what you're looking at and what you're getting into when buying one, which is where this chapter comes in.

CHECK YOUR NUMBERS

VW Beetles were fitted with a number of different size engines, starting with 1200cc, then 1300cc, 1500cc and 1600cc. VW very kindly stamped each and every engine they produced with an engine code, which you'll find in the metal of the alternator support flange. If this is obscured by oil and dirt, a wipe with a rag should reveal the numbers you are looking for.

The first letter in the sequence denotes the size of the engine and the information listed below will tell you what size it is, what model of VW it was fitted in (Type 1 Beetle, Type 2 Bus or Type 3) and what year VW fitted them.

VW ENGINE CODES

A 1200 Type 1 >'65
B 1600 Type 1 >'68–'70 / Type 2 '67–'70
C 1600 Type 2 '67–'70
D 1200 Type 1 '65>/Type 2 '59>
E 1300 Type 1 '65–'70
F 1300 Type 1 '65–'70
G 1500 Type 2 >'65
H 1500 Type 1 '65–'70/Type 2 '65–'68/Type 181 '69–'71
K 1500 Type 3 '65–'73
L 1500 Type 1 '66–'70/Type 2 '65>
M 1500 Type 3 '65–'73
N 1500 Type 3 '65–'73
P 1600 Type 3 '65–'73
R 1500 Type 3 '63–'65
T 1600 Type 3 '65–'73
U 1600 Type 3 '65>
UO 1600 Type 3 '67–'73
AB 1300 Type 1 '70–'73
AC 1300 Type 1 '70–'75
AD 1600 Type 1 '70–'73/Type 2 '70–'73
AE 1600 Type 1 '70–'71
AF 1600 Type 1 '70–'79/Type 2 '70–'79/Type 181 '74–'82
AG 1600 Type 181 '70–'76
AH 1600 Type 1 '71–'76
AJ 1600 Type 1 '74–'80
AK 1600 Type 1 '72–'73
AL 1600 Type 181 '73–'79
AR 1300 Type 1 '73–'75
AS 1600 Type 1 '73–'80/Type 2 '73–'80
ACD 1600 Type 1 '92–'04

The 'F' stamped in the case denotes this to be a 1300cc engine produced between 1965 and 1970 and a later addition to our 1958 Beetle.

SINGLE OR DUAL PORT?

You'll often hear people talking about an engine being a single or dual port engine. They are wondering if an engine has single or dual port cylinder heads. You can tell if the one you're looking at is a single or dual port engine by examining the intake manifold.

A single port manifold is, as the name suggests, a single piece of pipe that runs from the base of the carburettor into the cylinder heads on either side of the engine.

A dual port manifold has cast aluminium sections with two separate tubes that are bolted between the spark plugs where they enter the cylinder heads. If an engine doesn't have a manifold fitted, there will either be one or two holes in the top of the head depending on whether it's a single or dual port head. Easy really.

VW switched from single to dual port engines in 1971, as they offered more power, and you can buy kits to upgrade

This period-correct 30bhp engine was bought for the project car featured in this book, but things like the tinware, exhaust and distributor will all need addressing.

Single-port manifold.

Dual-port manifold.

an engine from single to dual port specification that come with new cylinder heads, manifolds and tinware.

IS IT COMPLETE?

If you're considering buying a replacement engine at a swap meet or from a private seller, how much of an engine are you getting for your money? Is it just a long block or is a complete unit, with the exhaust, heat exchangers, carburettor, tinware, clutch, and so on? Missing or worn-out parts will affect the price and can be an expensive pain to track down and replace, especially with older 30bhp and even earlier engines. That said, if you already have all these bits from another engine, there is little point paying for items that you won't need. Hence, a lot of people simply buy a replacement long block and transfer all their ancillaries over. This is fine, as long as you are replacing like for like and your existing components have plenty of life left in them.

CHECK THE OIL

The oil can tell you a lot about an engine. If it's thick and gloopy the owner hasn't changed it as often as they should have or looked after it properly. If it has a metallic shimmer it means there's metal in the oil, which points to worn bearings, or worse. Engines that have been stored for a period of time should have been done so with oil in them, as if not this can lead to corroded internals, which is never a good thing.

Oil leaks

A smattering of dirt and oil is perfectly acceptable on a secondhand engine, but significant leaks should be a cause for concern. Where it's leaking from can be a cheap and easy fix or a great deal more involved and, therefore, expensive. Should you discover an oil leak it could be a simple case of replacing whichever seal it is leaking from. For example, oil weeping from the bottom of the fan-shroud could indicate a blown oil cooler seal. Pop the fan-shroud off, remove the cooler, replace the seals and job done.

VW engines can have many leaks; this mess was caused by a leaky pushrod tube.

Fresh, clean oil. Perfect.

Flywheel oil seal

A leaking flywheel oil seal is a more complicated matter. It's arguably the one oil leak you least want to discover.

Have a look at the back of the engine. The flywheel is the large, circular piece of metal with all the teeth around the edge. The clutch bolts to this and the flywheel itself is bolted to the crank. It has an oil seal that prevents oil from the rear main bearing from leaving the case. These can dry out and split over time, usually if a car has been left to sit for a long period. Firing it back up into action can tear a dried-out seal and when that happens, the engine develops a massive oil leak.

A major loss of oil like this is messy, expensive and will kill an engine if you run it without any oil inside. It can also saturate the clutch and ruin it. If your clutch slips it's probably the result of a leaky flywheel oil seal. It should also be pointed out that another reason the seals wear out is because of end float, which is excessive play in the crankshaft.

Oil leaking from behind the flywheel means the main seal needs replacing. Worse, you could have play in the crank.

Grab the bottom pulley and try to move it in and out. Movement here means you have big problems with your engine.

END FLOAT

This is one of the first things you should check for on any engine as it's one of the more serious and expensive faults. If you find an engine with end float you are looking at a full tear down and rebuild and potentially having to throw the case and crank away and start again. All engines require various amount of clearance between components. If they didn't have any clearance they would seize up as soon as they warmed up.

The clearance of the crankshaft back and forth inside the case is known as end float. This measures between 0.07 and 0.13mm, which is just enough to feel but not enough movement to see. The way to check for end float is to grasp the bottom pulley with both hands and pull/push it in and out. Any movement at all is too much and means the mating surface between the flywheel end bearing and the case has been smashed out of shape.

If you can't turn the bottom pulley at all, it means you have a totally seized engine and that's bad, very bad news.

CLUTCH AND FLYWHEEL

Clutches wear out over time but are an easy fix, although you do have to remove the engine from the car to change them. Buying a secondhand engine with a clutch still fitted can save a few pounds, assuming it's still got some life left in it. Flywheels are pretty robust items but come in a couple of different styles. There are flywheels for 6-volt cars and flywheels for 12-volt cars. You can tell the difference by counting the teeth. A 6-volt flywheel has 109 teeth and a 12-volt flywheel has 130.

If an older 6-volt Beetle has had its electrics upgraded from the factory 6-volts to the later specification 12-volts, the flywheel and starter motor should have been changed to reflect this. However, some owners simply continue to run their 6-volt starter motor with the extra voltage, the result being that the starter spins over superfast and starts your engine really quickly. The downside to this is that it can eventually burn the starter motor out and the starter gear can shoot out too quickly and too far into the flywheel, damaging the teeth and getting itself jammed.

It should also be pointed out that, as discovered with the project car for this book, you can't simply fit a 12-volt flywheel to an older 30bhp engine in the same way you can with say, an early 1960s 6-volt Beetle. 30bhp engines have a different crank, so you need to run the old 6-volt flywheel and either run the original starter motor until it gives up the ghost or change it for a 12-volt, but 6-volt sized starter motor.

Early-style clutch. Flywheels are different for 6- and 12-volt cars; if there is no clutch fitted check the mating surface for scoring or damage.

Later style clutch pressure plate.

Properly fitted and secured tinware. Lovely.

This is an ex-industrial engine and has a fan guard. Most Beetles don't have them so check for damage or debris here.

TINWARE

The metal tins that encase an air-cooled VW engine are essential for keeping the engine cool. They're designed to keep the hot air from the engine and exhaust out of the engine bay. All of the components should be present, not bent out of shape and properly fastened down.

COOLING FAN

The largest piece of tinware is actually the fan shroud. This has a cooling fan inside that runs off the back of the dynamo/alternator. These in turn are run off the bottom pulley by the fanbelt. If the fanbelt snaps the dynamo/generator won't turn, which means the car's electrical

system won't charge. Worse still, if the dynamo/generator isn't turning, the cooling fan isn't either. This means your engine will overheat and a cooked engine is a dead engine. Look in the back of the fan shroud and ensure all the blades are intact. Sometimes they can be broken or blocked up by something that has been sucked in by the fan.

CARBURETTOR

Carburettors can cause all manner of running issues and have been known to cause engine fires. Spindles and seals wear over time, so give the throttle shaft a little wiggle and check for play. Check everything is free and moves as it should too.

It may look disgusting, but all this carb needed was a strip down, clean and replacement gasket.

This is an early dynamo, but a lot of people upgrade to a larger and more efficient alternator.

DYNAMO/ALTERNATOR

You can't really check these components unless the fanbelt has been removed or the engine is running. However, if you can, give the dynamo a spin and listen for a grating sound, which could indicate worn bearings and is usually the result of an overtight fan-belt.

DISTRIBUTOR

Decent replacements are getting hard to find and a lot of modern offerings have a bad reputation. Finding a good original dizzy on an engine is a bonus. Pop the cap off and have a look inside to check for rust and that the shaft doesn't have any play.

EXHAUST/HEAT EXCHANGERS

Quality replacements aren't cheap and cheap replacements aren't good, so if a replacement engine comes with a good, useable exhaust system it will save you a few pounds. Back boxes rust out over time, especially if a car has only been used for lots of short journeys. Heat exchangers are an air-cooled VW's heating system. Any leaks, holes, gaps or missing components will affect how much heat they generate, if any. Some owners remove the heat exchangers entirely and fit J-tubes. This can improve performance but means you get zero heat in the winter. This is worth bearing in mind if you plan to drive your VW in the colder months.

A standard vacuum advance distributor, with the vacuum canister on the side. You can suck on these to see if they draw air, should you wish.

Stock Beetle exhausts vary in quality. Cheap ones don't fit and can be very difficult to install.

Early cars have stale-air heat exchangers; later engines, like this one, have a fresh-air heating system and parts are cheaper.

6.2 Removal

As has been stated elsewhere in this book, air-cooled engines are weird little beasts. Among one of their many quirks is that unlike the vast majority of cars that have an engine that comes out of the top, when you need to remove it a Beetle engine comes out of the bottom of the car. This means you don't need to buy or hire a specialist engine hoist to tackle the job as you

TOP: *There are many reasons for removing an engine, but doing it once takes the mystery out of it. Never do it alone – always have a friend to lend a hand.*

should already have all the equipment you need – a jack, a couple of axle stands and a few simple hand tools.

Do this job once and you will realize how easy it is to pop the engine out of a Bug. In fact, the current world record for removing a Beetle engine was set by three Australians in 2005. They managed a time of just one minute and six seconds.

Obviously, you shouldn't compare yourself to these three, but if you take your time, label everything so you know how it goes back and get your head around the task, you'll become faster and more adept at Beetle engine removal the more times you do it.

Why would you want to remove a Beetle engine? Even if yours is running like a Swiss watch now and you have no need to replace it, sooner or later you will have to pull the engine. For example, changing the clutch is a job that can only be tackled with the engine removed. You might have a leaking flywheel oil seal or have to remove the fan shroud. There are even people who pull the engine out just to make servicing and changing the spark plugs easier.

There's no point procrastinating any longer. Let's get involved, shall we?

JACKING UP

As we have already stressed, the engine in a Beetle has to come out of the bottom of the car. Split Screen Type 2s and Early Bay Windows have a removable valance that makes this job much easier, but more of that later.

The first step is to get the rear end of the car jacked up and supported on axle stands. You need a solid, smooth floor to carry out this task as the car needs to be safe for you to work under and the smooth floor makes dragging the engine out much easier.

Where to place the jack causes a bit of debate. The author would never try to jack a Beetle up using the factory jacking points. You never know how strong or rusted they are. You can put a jack straight through a rusty jacking point, so it's best to avoid the potential harm and damage to yourself and the car that this can cause.

You should never place the jack under the engine either and you definitely don't want the jack to come into contact with the sump plate.

Either lift the rear up one side at a time by placing the jack under the torsion bar housing, then placing an axle stand under the torsion bar and doing the other side, or slide a trolley jack under the front of the gearbox, where the 'Y' of the frame meets, and jack up there. Some people advocate placing a block of wood between the 'Y'-shaped frame horns, but it can be tricky to keep the wood in place. Do whatever works best for you, but take your time and ensure you are happy and safe to proceed at every step.

You need to chock the front wheels so the car can't roll in either direction and once it's in the air you should check them again to ensure they haven't moved.

Once you're happy with where you've placed the jack, lift the rear up and place your axle stands under the rear torsion bars. Make sure they are sitting straight and level so that they catch the torsion bar securely when you lower it down onto them. You should place them as far in towards the rear hubs as you can but make sure you have room to pull the jack out. There is a seam/rib around the torsion bar, so place your axle stand just to the side of it.

RAMPED UP

Because the project car used in this book was stock height at this point, it was possible to reverse the rear end up some ramps. These have the added bonus of hydraulic jacks to raise the car even higher once it is sitting on the top platforms. You may not have these, or your car might not run, in which case you can't drive it up ramps. Or, if your car has been lowered, the rear wings may catch on the ramps or the front end may drag on the floor due to the angle of the car. The project stock car used in this book was fine though, so that's how the rear end was raised.

Disconnect battery

There are a few wires that need disconnecting before the engine can be removed. The first and most important ones connect to the battery. You need to disconnect the battery

1. Take your time and jack up properly to avoid damaging your car and yourself.

2. Ramps are great, assuming your car is able to drive up them. Always chock the wheels and leave the car in gear to prevent it from moving.

Engine and Related Systems

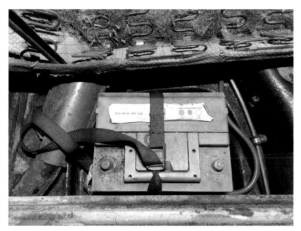

3. Remove the negative (-) terminal first, followed by the positive (+).
Reconnect in reverse order, positive (+) then negative (-).

before you do anything else. The battery can be found under the rear seat in a Beetle – and just the earth strap is fine – but it's good practice to remove both sides.

The negative terminal should be a black cable or a webbed metal strap that bolts to the frame. The positive should be a red cable, but it's not unheard of for people to fit whatever colour replacements they have to hand. Sometimes being cheap can be a real hazard.

When disconnecting a battery always remove the negative (-) terminal first, followed by the positive (+). Reconnect in reverse order, positive (+) then negative (-). By removing the negative first you're isolating the battery. If you tried removing the positive cable first and touched something like the metal seat frame with the spanner, you would witness some rather alarming sparks.

4. Familiarize yourself with the engine bay. It's pretty obvious what needs to come off once you have traced what goes where.

Electrical connections

There are a few wires that run to the engine and these need to be disconnected before the engine will come out. It's good practice to place a piece of masking tape around and label them. Take a picture on your phone if it helps you remember which wire goes where. They will either have push-on or screw-on terminals. For screw-on fixings, we recommend placing the screws back on the terminals to reduce the chances of losing them.

Oil sensor

To help you out, let's go through what has to come off. Start with the oil sensor. It should look like the one seen to the right and is located down by the distributor. This activates the oil warning light on the dash, so it's very important it goes back on when you refit the engine.

Dynamo/generator wiring

On a car with an alternator there is often a single, multi-point connector that just needs to be wiggled off. On an engine fitted with a dynamo, like the one featured in this book, there are two terminals that need to be removed. They're marked DF and D+ and you shouldn't get those confused, as one should have a spade connector and the other a ring

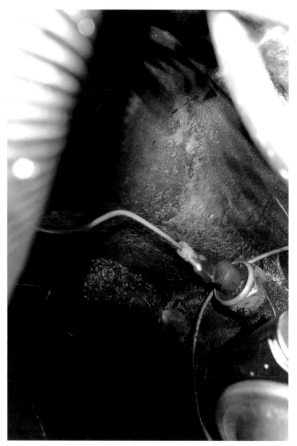

5. The ugly replacement terminal on the oil sensor is not ideal, but all the wiring in this car will eventually be replaced.

55

6. Place the nuts back on the terminals so you don't lose them.

connector. There is also a little earth connector that goes to the back. Remove all of them. There is usually an 8mm securing nut holding them on. Hold the back of the wire to prevent spinning the post and damaging the internal wiring.

Voltage regulator

These are either mounted on top of the dynamo or on the fan-shroud like in the car featured. There are two connections that need to be removed. Simply by tracing where it ran to, it was possible to see where the two heavy red wires needed to come off, followed by a thinner wire on the other side.

7. Take pictures, label wires, make diagrams. Do whatever you need to remember which wires go where.

8. You don't need to remove every wire and all cars are not the same. Use common sense and trace wires to see what needs to be removed.

Coil wires

The coil is the black canister usually mounted on the left side of the fan-shroud. It has positive and negative connections. Disconnect the wire to the positive side. The same wire runs to the right side of the carburettor, unless you have a manual choke. If there is one wire to the right side of the carburettor it's for the manual choke and needs to be disconnected. If there are two wires running to the carb the second is the electromagnetic cut-off jet. All of these connections are off-shoots of the same wire.

Throttle cable

There is a small cylindrical clamp that holds the cable end to the carb. Use a screwdriver or 8mm spanner to slacken it off enough to pull the cable out of the back. At this point, reach around the back of the fan-shroud and pull the throttle cable right the way back through the shroud. If you don't do it now, the chances are you will forget until you've got the engine balanced on the jack and half out of the car. That's never a good moment. Early cars have a manual choke, so there's another cable that runs from the dash to the carburettor. Remove that one as well and pull it back through the shroud for the same reason.

9. *Don't lose your throttle cable fittings. Place them in a bag, label them and store them somewhere you won't forget.*

10. *If you have an oil bath filter, try not to tip it to one side. That can be a messy mistake.*

Oil bath

The factory air-filter is the oil bath that sits on top of the carburettor. Some people replace this with an aftermarket paper type. Whatever style yours is, it needs to come off to give you extra clearance when you drop the engine. They're held in place by a single screw.

Air hoses

It depends on the year and design of your engine if you have air hoses running from the fan shroud to the lower

tinware. If you do, they need to come off. They should have clamps holding them in place, but these are often missing.

Front or back?

When discussing VW engines, the front and back of the engine is governed by a simple rule. Stand at the rear of the car and look at the engine. The back of the engine is the side facing you, towards the back of the car and the front is facing towards the front of the car. Simple enough. So, you need to remove the rear piece of tinware, the bit that goes under the bottom pulley and covers the exhaust.

11. *Air hoses are often ripped or damaged. Replacements are cheap, so change any that are in poor condition.*

12. You should have manifold clamps to remove, but those on the featured project car were missing.

13. The tinware should be held in place with a couple of crosshead screws.

Heater cables and hoses

If your car has its factory-fitted heater system, there will be a wire cable running to each of the heat exchangers and two flexible hoses that run into the body of the car to carry the heat. The hoses usually have just a simple push-on fitment, so they are easy to pop on and off. The heater cables attach to the heat exchangers with a cylindrical cable clamp, much like the one for the throttle cable. Slacken them off and the cables will slide out.

14. Heater hoses are a simple push on fit. Removing them is equally easy. Compress them and remove.

15. These are the fixings for the heat exchanger cables. If yours are not connected you won't have any heat in the car at all.

Fuel line

A Beetle's engine may be at the back of the car, but the fuel tank is all the way up in the front. Fuel runs from the tank along a metal line in the tunnel and is connected to the engine via a piece of rubber hose. You will need to disconnect the fuel line where it joins to the engine. Look underneath on the left-hand side and you'll see the line. It should be a rubber hose with two fuel clamps holding it in place. There may even be an in-line fuel filter plumbed in. If your car is going to be off the road for some time whilst you work on it, you could drain the tank. If not, remove the clamp nearest the engine and be ready to catch any fuel that spills out. Once the end is free, use a suitably sized screwdriver to plug the line and tighten the clamp. This should prevent any fuel leaking out. Double check there isn't any left in the line.

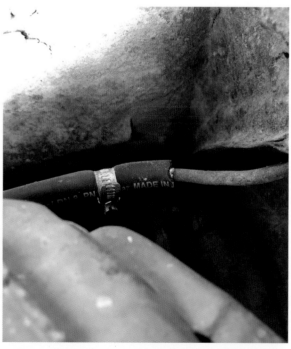

16. There is a hard fuel line that goes into a flexible hose down by the gearbox. Loosen the clamp and pop the line off.

17. Fuel line blocked off with a screwdriver. Sometimes a simple solution is all you need.

JUST FOUR BOLTS

One 'fact' you'll hear over and over again as a Beetle owner is that the engine is only held in by four bolts. Strangely enough, this is actually true – and now you are finally ready to tackle them. Two are accessed from below the car and to get to the other two you will need to stick your hand down the back of the fan-shroud. Tackle the bottom two first. Wriggle under the car and locate where the engine meets the gearbox. There are two nuts that attach to the lower engine studs. You

will need a 17mm socket/spanner to remove them. If they are not 17mm then they are not the nuts you're looking for. You'll probably need to clean a load of dirt and oil off them before removal, so a screwdriver/wire brush/rag is helpful. Give them a squirt of penetrating oil if you want to be sure they'll come out easily, leave them to soak and remove them.

At this point you need to place a jack under the engine to support it. Place a piece of wood between the jack and the bottom of the engine case and take care not to damage the sump plate.

Now you need to stick your arm down the back of the fan shroud and loosen the two remaining 17mm engine nuts. It is possible to see them if you look really hard behind the fan shroud, but you will do this job more by feel than anything else.

The bolt on the right of the engine holds the starter motor in place and the stud on the left is down by the clutch lever. Once all the nuts are removed, it's time for the engine to come out.

Place one hand on the fan shroud and another on the exhaust and wiggle, cajole and pull the engine towards you. You need to lift it and pull back at the same time, but take care not to wiggle it off the jack.

The tricky part is getting the engine to clear the input shaft in the gearbox bell housing, but it should come free. If it doesn't, make sure everything has been disconnected. It's easy to miss a wire, throttle or heater cable.

If the angle of the car makes it difficult to pull the engine free, dropping the back down a touch or raising the front up can help matters. Once the engine is off the input shaft you can carefully lower it down on the jack. When the jack is all the way down you need to tip the engine to one side

18. Ensure the engine is properly supported and there is no danger of the jack damaging anything vital, like the sump plate.

19. Not a job to tackle alone. There is a real sense of relief when the engine is finally on the ground.

20. With the engine removed you can clearly see the two lower engine studs and upper bolt holes either side of the flywheel.

21. Pop the bumper off, remove the valance and wheel the engine out. This modification makes a lot of sense.

and pull the jack out from underneath and, if there's room, slide the engine out from beneath the car. If the back end is too low, jack it up a little and then slide it. Some people remove one of the rear wheels to give themselves more room to pull it out.

Those four bolts

In the picture above, you can clearly see the four mounting points where the engine bolts to the gearbox. There are two studs at the bottom, in the roughly 7 and 5 o'clock positions, and there are two holes that the top bolts go into at the 11 and 1 o'clock positions. In the middle, you can see the splines of the clutch plate that the input shaft has to slide in and out of.

WORK SMARTER

Not harder. Now that you've read about engine removal, or better still, tried it yourself, we'll share a little modification that will make the job a whole lot easier in future.

How about making the rear valance removable? Why would you do that? Because VW should have from the start. After all, in their infinite wisdom, Volkswagen blessed all early Type 2s with a removable valance, so why not the Beetle?

Being able to remove the rear valance makes pulling an engine out so much easier. You don't have to mess around with jacking the car up and pulling the motor out from below, you just remove the rear bumper, pop the rear valance off and wheel the engine straight out the back.

Rear wings

A little disassembly is required. Just the back bumper and rear wings. Start by disconnecting the wires to the taillights and then remove the wings. If the wings haven't been removed for some time, give all the fastenings a good soak with some penetrating fluid first. Seized bolts are not uncommon and Beetles like to rot in the areas around the wing bolts.

22. Breaking eggs to make an omelette. Once the valance is removable you won't have to remove the rear wings again.

23. Those little round circles are the spot welds. They'll have to come out.

Locate spot welds

Beetles were spot welded together in the factory and the rear valance is fixed to the rest of the bodywork in a couple of areas. With the wings removed you can locate the spot-welds. This job might not be as straightforward if someone has replaced the rear valance at some point in the car's past. If that turns out to be the case, you may have to contend with their workmanship.

Drill

A spot weld drill bit will only set you back a couple of pounds. They're better than a regular drill bit, as they're designed for the job at hand. Buy yourself a couple, just in case you break one. Go easy and just drill out the spot weld. You don't want to go through the inner wing panel that the valance attaches to if you can help it.

Other welds

There are a couple of little welds in the engine bay right where you see this one in the bottom-right image, plus another on the other side. These will also have to go away before the valance can come out. Again, remove the welds and give the valance a little wiggle to show where it's still attached.

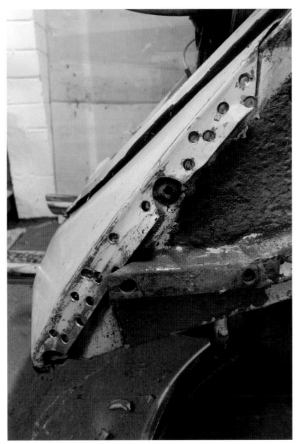

24. Once you have drilled out all the spot welds, you can peel back the flange. You will know if you have missed a weld at this point.

25. If your engine bay rubber has split like this, it's time to invest in a new one.

26. *Go easy with the chopping. Something small like a Dremel is ideal for detail work in tight areas.*

27. *Only one additional fastening is necessary. The wings sandwich the flange to hold it in place.*

The final cut

There is one last cut you have to make – well, two actually, as there's the other side and it looks like the top-left image. Once you've completed this task your valance should come out. You now need to come up with a way of re-attaching it.

Attachment issues

You need to come up with some fastenings that won't interfere with the rear wings. In the top-right picture you can see how we're using some of the wing bolts to hold the valance in place. The bottom and middle fastenings are regular wing bolts that sandwich the valance between the inner and outer wing. The top bolt has been added to bolt through the outer wing, inner wing and valance.

To remove the valance, you only have to loosen the bottom and middle bolt, but the top one you have to take right out.

You will need to paint where you have drilled the valance or rust will set in. For a really tidy job you could weld up the old spot-weld holes, but no one will see this when the wings are bolted on.

Like it never happened

No one would ever know the valance is now removable. Removing the engine now is simply a case of unbolting the rear bumper, removing the two retaining bolts we added to the valance and loosening the wing bolts and sliding it out. A little work now makes removing the engine an awful lot easier in the future.

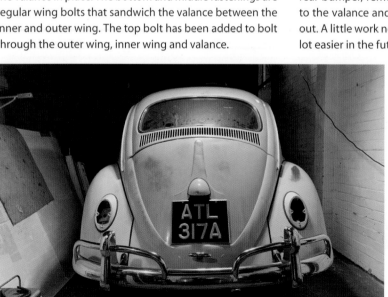

The best modifications are the ones that don't look like modifications at all.

6.3 Ancillaries: strip and clean

Just because something looks a bit old and tired, it doesn't mean it's no good. We live in a throwaway society, but that mentality won't do you any favours when it comes to old VWs. The simple fact of the matter is the vast majority of replacement parts you can buy today are inferior to factory originals.

If you take one piece of advice away from this book it would be to never change an original VW part for a new one unless you absolutely have to. Sure, that will annoy any of the VW parts specialists reading this, but ask anyone who has ever worked on a Beetle and they will agree: original VW is better than anything. End of story.

Take replacement tinware, for example. You would think tinware is tinware, right? Wrong. Cheap pattern replacements are a nightmare to fit. Nothing lines up as it should, you have screw holes where you don't need screw holes, gaps where there shouldn't be gaps and paying someone to fit reproduction tinware can be an expensive undertaking, as a lot of time and work goes into wrinkling out all of the faults.

TOP: *(left) The starting point was this former industrial engine, hence the fire-engine red paint on the lower tinware.*

TOP: *(right) The result after all the hard work. Not bad – and all it took was a little effort and some rattle cans.*

Then there are replacement exhausts. Try getting a cheap replacement back box to line up with the manifold and heat-exchangers and you will soon discover why people pay a premium for NOS (New Old Stock) parts or restore tatty original components instead.

Having removed and sold the later, 1300cc engine for this book's project car, a period-correct 1200cc was tracked down to replace it. Life would have been a bit easier if the 1200cc engine wasn't an early 30bhp engine, but the devil, as they say, is in the detail – and we wanted a period-correct engine for the car featured in this book.

The differences between a 30-horse 1200 and a later regular 1200cc engine are many, but essentially, the generator pedestal is part of the engine block casting. Later 1200cc engines have a bolt-on pedestal. They also come with a semi-automatic choke, whereas 30-horse versions have a manual choke cable. The heating system is different as well. The list is endless, but essentially it was impossible to buy a replacement 30bhp 1200 from a supplier in the way that you can a later 1200, 1300 or 1600 Beetle engine.

The starting point was an ex-industrial engine. Air-cooled flat fours were used for all manner of roles, such as stationary generators, or as in this case, as a water-pump for a local fire department. All of which explains the red paint and magneto rather than a conventional distributor.

The magneto would have to be replaced as they don't have the rev range of a distributor, which is fine on a stationary engine, but not what you need in a car that goes up and down the gears.

The really great thing about an engine like this is that it won't have seen much use. The one featured in this book had something like 150 hours of running time, which equates to about 14,500km (9,000 miles). For an engine that's 63 years old that's a little under 230km (143 miles) a year. So, it's essentially a brand-new engine.

The downside is… well, just look at it. There was no way it was going to be installed looking like that, and proper 30bhp parts are harder to come by and more expensive than later engine parts.

Just one more thing before you continue. You may be wondering why we don't go the whole hog and rebuild an entire engine for this book. Well, it's a more complicated task than there is room for here. Sure, you can throw an air-cooled flat four together from bits and bobs, but don't expect it to last long. If you know your way around an engine build this book probably isn't really for you anyway, and if you don't then we would recommend you go away and read up on what's involved in building an engine properly. Or, better still, enlist the help of an expert. There are many engine builders and suppliers of reconditioned units out there, so if you do need one, there are plenty to choose from. And, if you buy a replacement engine, at least now you will now know how to transfer all your old bits over to it. So, let's get started.

WORKBENCH

It helps if you can work somewhere with plenty of room, lots of light and your tools close to hand. Placing the engine on a bench like this also means you won't get back-ache from stooping over it for hours on end. Stripping an air-cooled engine down to a long block is an easy and surprisingly fun task. You will soon discover that they have to come apart in a certain order and building them up again, as the saying goes, is just the reversal of what you're about to see. Albeit, it's a lot nicer, as you are working with fresh, clean, new parts instead of gummed-up, rusted components.

Exhaust/heat exchangers

There wasn't a great deal left of the exhaust system in the featured car, but we started by removing that anyway. It was a jagged, rusty tetanus shot waiting to happen, but if you have a complete back box, the process is the same; remove the tinware screws to release the pulley tin and undo the 10mm bolts that attach the exhaust to the manifold. Then, remove the 14mm bolts that hold the heat exchangers to the engine. In this instance, the car had J-tubes, but the process is the same. If the nuts are rusty you may find they unwind the studs from the case. That's ok, you can remove the nut and then wind the stud back in once it's off the engine.

2. Soak any suspect-looking fastenings with penetrating fluid beforehand, because they will probably be rusted on.

1. A single person can lift a Beetle engine on their own, but do your back a favour and ask a friend to help out.

3. You may unwind the exhaust studs when you remove them. If so, remove the nuts and wind them back in again.

4. Getting to the rear nut can be a pain. If you're stripping the engine, removing the manifold with the carburettor still attached really helps.

5. Removed and ready for a strip and clean.

Remove carburettor

You can leave the carb bolted to the manifold and remove it as one piece, but as it's important to do this properly and this one needed cleaning, the carb was removed. It's held in place by two 13mm nuts. The one at the back is a little harder to get to, but once you get a spanner on it, it will come off easily enough. You can reuse the gasket if it's not damaged, but this one was split so needed replacing.

Top pulley

It's pretty obvious the fanbelt has to come off to remove the dynamo. The top pulley is actually made up of two pieces. To remove the front section, jam a screwdriver in one of the notches to lock it in place whilst using a 21mm socket to loosen the pulley nut. There will be a collection of shims inside that alter the tension of the belt. Put them

6. Loosen the top pulley nut and remove the fanbelt.

7. The more shims between the pulley halves, the slacker the fanbelt will be. Remove washers to tighten, add to loosen.

all back on the generator and secure with the pulley nut to stop you losing them.

Generator strap

The generator/dynamo is secured by a metal strap that runs under the pedestal. Remove the bolt clamping the two ends together and slide it out.

8. Placing nuts and bolts back inside components reduces the risk of losing them and reminds you how things go back together.

9. Don't forget to fit the generator strap and secure with the nut and bolt.

Fan shroud

You will find a crosshead screw on either side of the fan shroud. Remove them with a tight-fitting screwdriver. There's an oil cooler in there and it's a snug fit, but give it a tug and it will lift free.

11. You can remove the generator from the fan shroud, or remove it as a complete unit as shown here.

Generator

The generator is held in the fan shroud by four bolts. Remove them and it will come free. The engine in the featured car was running 6-volt electrics, so a 12-volt replacement was found, complete with the correct tinware, so it didn't need stripping down any further.

10. Two little screws are the only things holding the fan shroud in place. There is one on either side.

12. *Removing the generator is as simple as removing the four bolts in the generator backing plate and pulling it free.*

13. *That fan cools your engine. If it sucks anything in to stop it rotating or it snaps the blades, you will cook your motor very quickly.*

Remove manifold

The inlet manifold is attached to each cylinder head by two nuts. Pop them off and the manifold will come free. The featured engine had a cool guide tube for the plug wires to run through, but when a wire wheel was run over the manifold it was obvious it had rotted through. This is a pretty common occurrence and someone adept at metalwork would be able to repair it. In this case a spare from the stash of parts was fitted instead.

15. *This heat riser/manifold has a cool guide tube to hide the HT wires. Two screws hold it in place.*

14. *Four 10mm nuts secure the heat risers to the heads.*

16. A common problem with manifolds. It looked okay, but the metal had thinned, and holes appeared when the wire wheel was run over it.

Cylinder-head tins

There are a number of screws dotted around holding the tinware in place. It's a good idea to soak them in penetrating oil before you poke a screwdriver in one. Some can be stuck fast. They can generally be shaken free, though.

18. VW tinware is just a 3D metal jigsaw and should all slot together perfectly.

Degrease and clean

The featured engine was covered in years of grime. It could not be left like that, so it was carefully protected and given a thorough clean.

17. Seized screws are not uncommon. Don't destroy the heads; breakout the impact screwdriver and shock them free.

19. When cleaning an engine, plug any holes and cover anything you don't want water to enter.

20. If you don't have any specific engine degreaser to hand, you can just use oven cleaner and give it a scrub.

Blocked manifold?

Over time, carbon builds up in the heat risers, which eventually blocks them. When that happens, it can lead to poor running and your car cutting out until it's had time to warm up. The accepted way to unclog a blocked manifold is to run a hefty wire through it with a drill. Otherwise, intense heat followed by rapid cooling can help to dislodge stubborn carbon. Try putting the manifold on a hot barbeque, then rinsing it with cold water. Using the drill again should then run it through clear.

22. The author came up with this fix himself. The thinking was that the heat would expand the metal and loosen the carbon that had built up inside.

23. This is all that could be broken free with the drill and wire.

21. Running a length of wire through the manifold with a drill is the usual way to unclog a blocked one.

24. This is what came out after it had been thrown on the barbeque.

GOOD AS NEW

You could spend money hand over fist and simply replace any part that doesn't cut the mustard, or you could save yourself a few pennies and get some pleasure from restoring old components. This rusty back box came off another car long since sold. It was rusty but it is solid and, being an original VW part, is much better quality than a modern replacement. The surface rust was cleaned off with a wire wheel on the end of the drill and it was then painted in heat-resistant paint.

Never throw anything away. This old exhaust is an original VW part and it's a better fit than any modern repro.

It just needed the surface rust knocking off with a wire wheel.

After a few coats of high-temperature exhaust paint. Not bad.

GO THE EXTRA MILE

For the best results you need to invest a little time and effort into your work. Don't be tempted to cut corners or rush jobs, because you run the risk of making a hash of things. Details like paintwork can really make or break a car and you need to invest a little time in the prep work. Sand things down to ensure there's a good, flat surface, key and prime everything properly so the topcoat has a better chance of sticking and remove or mask up details to achieve the best results possible.

The generator should have been removed from the backing plate, but it was masked up instead.

Do the job right and do it once. Take your time and, if you're not happy, do it again.

A decent finish is all in the prep. Mask up or ideally remove as many pieces as you can prior to painting.

Celebrating a job well done. Arguably, other beverages are more suitable to the garage environment.

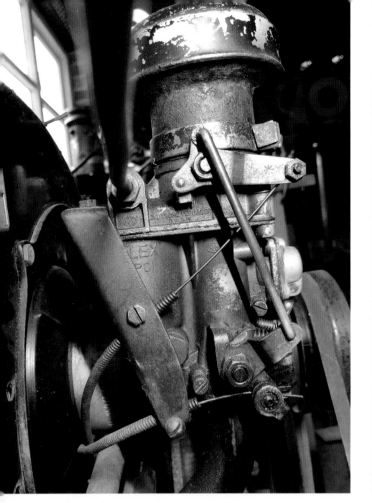

6.4 Carburettor

Solex were the go-to carburettors for VW during the air-cooled years. Find anything else in your Beetle's engine bay and you will know it's an aftermarket addition. Style and size varied over the years, but the principles are the same for whatever carb you're faced with. What we suggest you do is to have a read through this guide and then go online and search for a diagram of your specific carb. You'll find one easily enough and they are an invaluable reference tool.

A lot of people are scared of digging into a carburettor, but stripping one down is simplicity itself. That said, they are precision instruments and you do need to pay attention to what you are doing. Every jet and washer has an important part to play and should you miss one out your engine won't run as it should. More seriously, you could end up with a fuel leak and that could lead to the most major of catastrophes – an engine fire.

Replacement carbs are readily available but so are rebuild kits for most carbs from the 1960s onwards and

they are a good deal cheaper. A rebuild kit usually contains all the gaskets, seals, washers and jets you need to overhaul your carburettor.

Being for a late 1950s 30-horse engine, the 28 PCI carb shown here is a little rarer, so parts are harder to come by. The dedicated rebuild kit bought from a well-known VW parts specialist actually contained none of the bits needed, so it was necessary to track down new seals and gaskets as you really should replace the old ones when carrying out an overhaul like this. The only part that was hard to track down was the correct carburettor body gasket, which eventually surfaced in the USA on the ever-useful thesamba.com website.

ORIENTATION

Having given the outside a thorough degrease whilst it was still on the car, it was removed from the manifold (just two 13mm nuts, remember?) and transferred to a clean working environment (the dining room table) where it would be clear if anything dropped off.

Take as long as you need to familiarize yourself with how everything goes together. Use your phone or a digital camera and take as many pictures as you need, showing it as a complete unit and all the stages of deconstruction. Knowledge, as they say, is power – but if you begin to feel out of

TOP: *(left) The starting point was the 28 PCI carburettor from the project car's 30bhp industrial engine. It was dirty but in otherwise good condition and ran well.*

TOP: *(right) The same carburettor, cleaned up and fitted with an NOS oil bath air-filter and restored manifold.*

1. *Degreased to make work a little more pleasurable. Taking photos on your phone will help when you come to reassemble.*

your depth there is no shame in handing the job over to a specialist.

DIGGING IN

The carb on the featured car came off an ex-industrial engine and had this nifty little bracket for the throttle and choke cables, so the job started with that. As stated earlier, not all carbs are the same, but the principles of working on them are. Just remember how things come off and in what order you removed them.

2. *Soaking everything with penetrating oil first is a smart move – you don't want to force anything and cause any damage.*

Upper body assembly

The top has to come off first. Later carbs have a semi-automatic choke, but this one has a manual choke with a linkage that had to come off before anything else. An 11mm spanner was the perfect tool for the two retaining nuts.

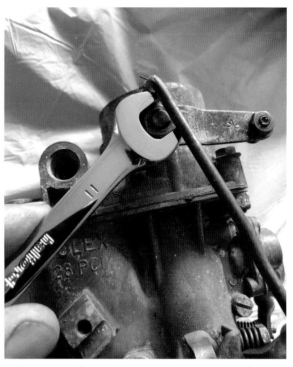

3. *Always use snug-fitting tools to prevent damaging screw heads and other fixings. Nothing says 'uncaring owner' like rounded-off heads.*

4. *All carburettors are essentially the same and it is pretty obvious how they come apart. Taking photos will help with assembly.*

5. The model-specific rebuild kit we ordered came with totally the wrong gasket, so we bought an original one from America.

6. If the float sticks or sinks in the carburettor, it can overflow with fuel and cause a fire – so it's a simple, but crucial, component.

7. The way to test a float for holes is to pop it in a bowl of water. If it stays on the surface, it's good to go again.

Carb body gasket

With the four retaining screws and top removed it was possible to see inside. The gasket was very thin and

brittle and a replacement was in order. The old one was used as a handy reference guide, as there are all manner of carbs and gaskets out there. It was then stored away safely in the spare parts stash. You never know when you might need something, even if it is just for reference or as a quick fix.

Float

The carb float is held in place by a brass pin. The float simply lifts out and the lever slides out of the bracket. The float needs to do exactly as its name suggests. To do so it needs to be airtight and you can check this simply enough by popping it in a bowl of water. If it floats, it's good.

Float chamber

As suspected, the bottom of the float chamber was full of old fuel residue and dirt. This is exactly the sort of stuff that will block a jet and causes running issues. Definitely time for a clean.

Brass jets

These are pretty delicate, so you need to be careful when removing the brass jets from a carb. Always use a well-fitting screwdriver and if you come across a stubborn one, use penetrating fluid and give it a little time to work its magic.

8. *Not an old ashtray, but the insides of an old carb that hasn't been used for a while.*

10. *We found a model-specific diagram online that helped with reference and naming all the parts that come off.*

9. *For a full strip and clean you just need to go around removing and storing everything carefully.*

11. *To clean a carburettor properly, it all has to come apart.*

Go steady

The carrier main-jet was pretty stubborn, probably as a result of being in there for quite some time, dirt and a strong-wristed former keeper. A little WD40 and a snug spanner helped winkle it out.

Count the turns

Idle mixture and speed screws need to be removed and cleaned. It's important these passageways are cleaned and blown through with compressed air to remove all traces of dirt and debris.

12. When removing these, count and make note of how many turns they are from fully wound-in and reinstall them the same way.

Clean and soak

These are all the brass fittings that came out of the carb. Everything was sprayed down with carb cleaner and left to soak overnight. You need to soak everything long enough for the cleaner to do its thing. You can leave them to soak

13. As you can see, everything was pretty filthy. Pop it all straight in a jar or tub to avoid losing any of it.

14. We gave everything a good blast with carb cleaner.

15. Leaving the brass components to soak in Cola overnight brought them up like this.

in malt vinegar or Cola as the acidity in either will remove all of the tarnish.

Compressed air

When you are happy with how clean everything is, it's time to reassemble. Just reverse the steps you took to take

16. If you don't have a compressor at home, one of those cans of air you can buy for cleaning computer keyboards will help.

17. Use a good-quality penetrating lubricant and check everything operates as it should.

it apart and fit new gaskets where appropriate. Once the body of the carb is clean, give all of the passageways a blast of compressed air. This should remove any traces of dust/debris/dirt.

Lubrication

Having cleaned all of the gunk and grime off your carb it's a good idea to lubricate all of the moving parts to ensure free and easy movement.

ADJUSTING

With the carb refitted it's time to give it a little fettling. There are many things that can make an engine run poorly, so give yourself a good head start and ensure you've correctly gapped the points, sparkplugs and your timing is correct. That way, you'll know anything you do now is purely down to carburettor adjustment. If all of that is fine and you reset the mixture screws to how they were before you stripped the carb, the engine should start. The engine needs to be

18. This is a later 34 PICT 3 carburettor, as it is more representative of what you will have to play with, but the following method is essentially the same for all carbs.

19. Most owners try to sort running issues with the idle control. That is not the right way to do it.

20. Go slow and be patient. It takes time for the engine to respond to any inputs.

warm, so leave it running for a bit or take it for a quick spin around the block if you can. Once it's warmed up enough to be 'off-choke' you can begin fine tuning.

Throttle-adjusting screw

A lot of owners only ever tinker with the throttle-adjusting screw to speed up the idle. This isn't good. You should leave it at the factory settings so that the engine ticks over somewhere around 800–900rpm. You will need a rev counter (something a Beetle doesn't have) or timing light to really do this properly. To reset yours, wind it anti-clockwise until the point no longer comes into contact with the stepped cam of the choke set-up. Then, wind it back in so it just touches the cam and then give it one further quarter-turn clockwise.

Idle speed

The idle speed screw is usually the larger of the two brass screws (on the left side of the carb as you face it). In order to increase the rpm you wind the screw outwards (anti-clockwise) and in the opposite direction to slow it down again.

Mixture

Wind the mixture screw inwards (clockwise) until the revs begin to drop and then back it out again (anti-clockwise) until the revs begin to increase again. Stop when the revs stop increasing and wind it back until you notice a slight drop, then back it out a final quarter turn and you should be all set.

21. A timing light really comes in handy for this, but a lot of owners learn to do it by ear and feel.

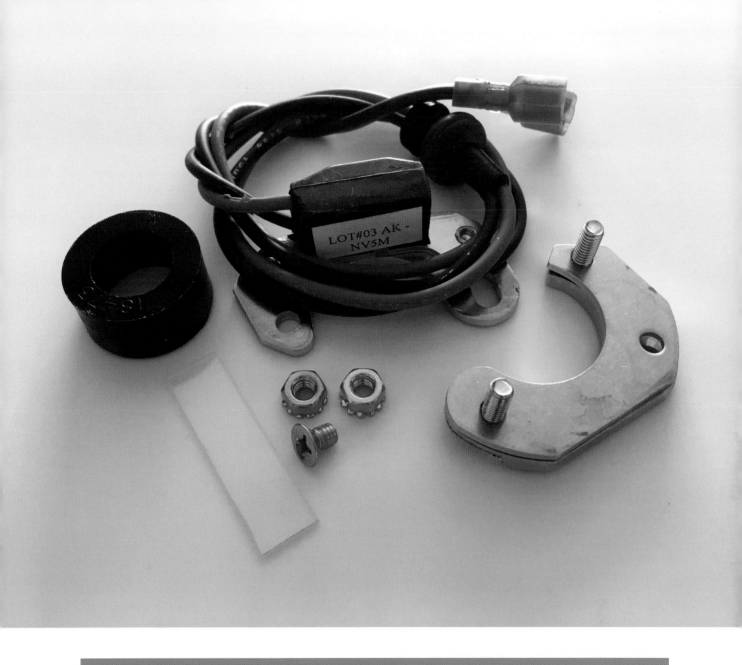

6.5 Electronic ignition

Type the words 'electronic ignition' into any dedicated VW forum and you'll see people fall into two distinct categories, the lovers and the haters. Some people argue the quality of these kits leaves a lot to be desired. They say that in their experience, the kits they've fitted have only lasted a few hundred miles before breaking down and they've reverted back to the old points and condenser set-up. Personally, the author has never had any issues with running electronic ignition on any air-cooled VW and would argue it's the best £100 you can spend on your car.

Ninety per cent of the breakdowns the author has suffered have been linked to the electrical system, with the condenser being the main offender. You know there's an issue brewing with one of those little blighters when your car becomes sluggish to start and the engine develops a stutter. When it finally decides to quit entirely, you have an engine that won't fire at all.

Doing away with the points and condenser means eliminating two of the weakest points in the chain, the condenser and the points, which can close up or corrode. Fitting an electronic ignition also means you never have to worry about the points gap again.

That said, for peace of mind, always carry a spare set of points and a condenser with you. That way, if you are unlucky enough to experience issues, you can always go back to the factory set-up.

TOP: *Wave goodbye to setting points gaps and dodgy condensers by upgrading to electronic ignition.*

WHICH KIT?

There are a number of kits available that will allow you to upgrade a Beetle to electronic ignition. Some are cheap and nasty, others are decidedly more expensive. You will also find variants designed to work on vacuum and non-vacuum advance distributors and both 6- and 12-volt cars. So, take your time, do your research and make sure you buy the right one for your car.

The kit shown at the start of this section is a Pertronix; it costs around £100 and is one of the more commonly fitted kits. Again, people either love them or loathe them, so you make your choice and you pay your money.

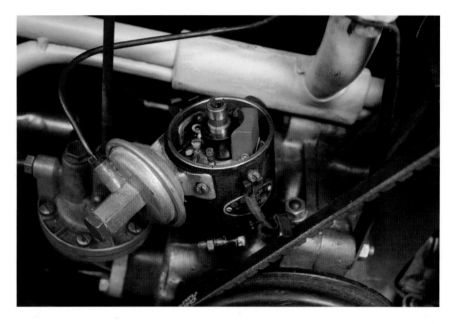

This kit is designed for a 6-volt car with a vacuum advance distributor, which proves you can upgrade any Beetle to electronic ignition.

First thing to do – after you have checked you've got the right kit for your engine – is to pop your dizzy cap off and remove the rotor arm. You will reuse those bits so make sure they're still healthy, with no signs of cracks, splits or wear. Just place or wedge the distributor cap out of the way, rather than pulling all of the HT leads off. If you leave them all connected you won't get yourself in a pickle with the firing order and potentially blame the new ignition module if the engine doesn't start or runs poorly once you have fitted everything.

This is a 1600cc engine with an 009 mechanical advance distributor, but the process is the same for any dizzy.

1. Pop the old points and condenser in your glove box or spares box, as you never know if you might need them again.

2. Leave the condenser wire attached to the coil if it helps you remember which side is the negative (-).

Points and condenser

Remove both of these but be careful not to drop the screws and washers. The green wire from the condenser runs to the negative (-) side of the coil. Either leave it attached for now or make a note of which side it went to; it's important to know which side of the coil is positive (+) and which is negative (-). You'll see why in a minute.

Install module

Depending on which kit and distributor you have there should be a base plate that goes in first. Fix it down with the crosshead screw that comes in the kit, fit the module and run the coil wires through the body of the distributor.

Magnetic sleeve

There is a magnetic sleeve that slides down the distributor shaft and onto the cam. It has to be properly seated on the cam, but you'll feel it go on. The bottom edge of the sleeve has to sit level with the bottom edge of the ignition module. If it doesn't, your kit may include a spacer, which you'll have to fit.

3. Don't fully tighten the module down just yet as you need to set the gap.

4. The sleeve needs to sit at the right height on the cam. If it doesn't, go back a step and fit the spacer plate.

Set the gap

To ensure the gap is properly adjusted, the kit should contain a little plastic feeler gauge. Slide it between the

module and the sleeve and tighten the base plate up once you're happy the gap is correctly set.

Coil wires

Check the coil wires don't interfere with any moving parts and that the rubber grommet is properly seated. The next bit is crucial. Get it wrong and you will destroy the new ignition module before you've even driven out of the garage. The black ignitor wire has to go the negative (-) side of the coil and the red wire goes to the positive (+) side of the coil. There is usually a warning on the box saying that if you get this wrong, it's your fault and there are no comebacks. That's it. Job done. You'll never have to set the points gap again, but we would recommend checking the timing once the engine has had a chance to warm up, just to ensure everything is running at its optimum level.

5. Take the opportunity to lubricate the cam through the felt wick whilst you are in there.

6. Run the wires through the body of the distributor and fit the rubber grommet to prevent any chafing.

7. Don't get the wires mixed up or you will immediately destroy the module.

6.6 Starter motor

Starter motors are one of those items you take for granted. You turn the key and your engine starts. Until one day, it doesn't…. The tell-tale sign your starter has gone bad is if you turn the key and are greeted by the sound of silence, or just a simple click. The problem usually lies with the solenoid, which is the cylinder on the side of the unit that is energized by a coil drawing power from the ignition circuit.

A push start or slithering under the car to give the starter a few taps with a hammer can often get you out of trouble, but it's not a long-term fix.

If this happens to you, ensure the battery terminals are clean and tight, the battery has enough charge and the connections on the back of the starter are also clean and tight.

You may come up against a stuck Bendix. This is when you hear the starter spinning but it doesn't actually start the car. This means the Bendix isn't engaging with/spinning the flywheel. This can also be traced back to the solenoid or a worn starter-motor bush in the bellhousing.

A less common fault is the starter motor continues to spin after you've started the engine and released the ignition key. This usually means the contacts in the solenoid have fused together and the battery is still sending power to the starter motor.

TOP: *The starter motor bolts to the gearbox, on the right-hand side of the car as you face the back of the car.*

The starter passes through the bell-housing and spins the flywheel on the back of the engine.

A replacement starter motor with a new bushing for the bell-housing.

6.7 Troubleshooting/won't start

There are many reasons why a car can be fine one day but refuse to start the next. However, most of the time, it will drop a few hints that something is rotten in the state of Denmark – you just need to keep an eye and an ear out for them and

TOP: *Simple technology means simple fixes when something does go wrong.*

whatever you do, don't ignore them, as you can guarantee you'll break down at the most inconvenient time and place imaginable.

What are the little tell-tale signs, you ask? There are so many, but one example would be something like a slight stutter whilst driving. This points to there being an issue about to raise its ugly head. It could be dirty fuel and a blocked jet in the carb, so ask yourself if you have run the car low on fuel lately? Rust and sediment in the bottom of a tank can get sucked into the carb and ruin play. Hence, it's good practice to always have at least a quarter of a tank when driving a classic car.

If it's not the fuel then it will be something wrong with the electrical system, most likely the points or condenser. The author always carrys spares of those and once he has eliminated the possibility of loose wires or a connection that may have popped off, these are the first things he checks or replaces. Especially condensers. For some reason they

often go bad and the tell-tale sign, as we've mentioned, is just a slight stutter once or twice, but then you know bad times are coming and it's time to replace it.

When a car won't start it really is just a process of elimination. Work through the steps and you will get to the root of the problem. If you have a few hand tools and spare parts, you will be back on the road in no time. The best advice is always start with the obvious and easy stuff and then go from there.

A few of the most common faults and the culprits behind them are listed in the section below.

STARTING PROBLEMS

Engine turns over but won't fire

1. Flat battery.
2. Points gap is dirty, pitted or out of adjustment.
3. Faulty condenser.
4. Faulty coil or wire to condenser.
5. Distributor cap dirty or cracked.
6. Brush inside distributor cap not coming into contact with rotor arm.
7. Rotor arm is worn or damaged.
8. Blown or loose fuse.
9. Run out of petrol.
10. Dirty fuel has clogged the fuel line or carburettor.
11. Fuel pump is broken – tap with hammer or replace.
12. Faulty ignition switch.

Engine won't turn over

1. Flat battery.
2. Starter motor/solenoid – try putting car in gear and rock back and forth and try again or tap the starter with a hammer.
3. Engine is totally seized (worse-case scenario).

Engine runs but misfires

1. Check points, distributor cap, for loose wires (coil wire).
2. Spark plug/HT leads breaking down.
3. Loose spark plugs or HT leads.
4. Spark plug gap incorrectly set.
5. Ignition timing too far advanced or retarded.
6. Dirt in the carburettor.

6.8 Modifications/upgrades

The air-cooled flat four is a wonderful piece of engineering. It was designed to be cheap to build, easy to work on, frugal to run and reliable. When properly maintained these engines will happily chirp along at their top speed for hours at a time and can rack up serious mileage.

One thing they are not, however, is fast. As far as that goes, you have two options. You can accept it as part of the Beetle's charm, or you can invest some time, money and effort into making your car quicker. The only limiting factor is your budget. If you are willing to spend big, you can turn a Beetle into something that will traumatize the boy racers at the traffic lights.

Fast Beetles are a big deal. Ever heard of Cal Look? It's a term that originated in the 1960s and can be traced back to a few guys in a Californian VW club who reworked their Beetles to keep up with and embarrass the homegrown muscle cars of the era. Cal Look cars traditionally have large-capacity engines, a nose-down stance, after-market

wheels and the trim and bumpers are deleted in the pursuit of cleaner lines and a few extra horsepower.

The thing is, you don't have to go the whole hog and build a Cal Looker to have a Beetle with more poke. There are plenty of things you can do to squeeze a few extra ponies under the bonnet, and should you require a replacement engine or rebuild, this could be the perfect time to do precisely that.

For the purposes of this section the lovely people at the VW Engine Company (www.thevwenginecompany.com) offered their expert advice. They are engine specialists who have been around for decades. Both their engines and customer service are highly recommended.

When asked what to do with a tired out air-cooled flat four the VW Engine Company said it is important to note that a repair is generally just a short-term fix. For long-term peace of mind, you should really be looking at a full strip down and reconditioning service from a reputable engine company – one that guarantees its work.

Engine-building itself is a bit of a dark art. Go online and the amount of advice from DIY builders can be quite bewildering; hence, we recommend utilizing the services of a dedicated specialist.

TOP: *Nothing too wild – just a 1641cc with twin carbs – but it allows the car to keep up with traffic, is reliable and returns decent mpg.*

Matching numbers cars are always worth a premium. So long as it's not worn beyond repair, having your original engine rebuilt is a smart move.

Sure, you can throw an engine together using whatever old parts you have lying around the garage, but don't expect it to last long and be trouble-free whilst it is in use.

You need to do things properly and reconditioning does not mean just rebuilding. All of the VW Engine Company's engines are completely stripped, inspected, tested, machined and re-assembled using brand new components, including piston and liners, cylinder heads, and so on. It's the only way to ensure reliability and longevity.

If your engine is worn out and needs replacing, you have two options available to you:

LIKE-FOR-LIKE ENGINES

This is the most cost-effective route if you need a replacement engine, and so long as all ancillaries are serviceable and in place, including all of the cooling tins, then everything can be transferred over to the replacement engine. The VW Engine Company can rebuild a customer's own unit where possible, which is a real bonus for those wanting to maintain originality and matching numbers.

UPGRADING

Taking this route will give you more power and make the car more comfortable to drive, but it will come at a higher cost. Precisely how much comes down to the number of components from your old engine that can be re-used, and this is something a decent engine specialist can advise on.

With the VW Engine Company's range of Type 1 engines, they can even supply an engine built with a brand-new crank case. They like to keep within their chosen specs as they are tried and tested, but they can also offer adaptations such as full-flow oil systems, for example, and build to a personal specification.

The VW Engine Company also offers a full turnkey service, as well as full supply and fit. Or for anyone wanting to have an engine fitted elsewhere, they can provide support and guidance as well as full running in, care and mainte-

If you are still not up to the challenge, find a trusted specialist who can build, install and fine-tune an engine for you.

nance advice. Great piece of mind if you feel working on a Beetle's engine is still a little beyond your capabilities.

Larger capacity

Many owners go looking for increased torque and performance. If you're only after a little more grunt up hills, then a 1600cc with twin carbs and a better exhaust will feel a great deal livelier than a 1200cc or 1300cc.

If you're rebuilding a 1600cc then you can up the capacity to 1641cc for just a few extra pounds, but many people say there is no noticeable difference in power and you're actually compromising the engine by running thinner cylinder

A VW Engine Co. 1776cc with twin 40 IDF Weber carbs, their go-to carburettors. It is also running a Vintage Speed exhaust and Pertronix distributor.

walls, as the engine will run hotter. That said, 1641cc is a very popular engine size and you will notice the difference if you also upgrade to twin carbs, a better exhaust, cam and rockers.

Basically, the more brake horsepower you chase the more it will cost you in performance parts and the more looking after the engine will require. You are also more likely to encounter problems using it on a regular basis.

You have to really want to live with a fast VW engine and be willing to put in the time to maintain it.

A great many owners who go down the fast VW route ultimately end up returning to stock in the end. Overheating, running issues and the need to keep things like twin carbs in balance eventually outweigh the need for speed. So, whilst engines like the commonly seen 1835cc, 1914cc and 2007cc are more exciting to drive, they are certainly not for everyone.

The VW Engine Company's biggest seller in terms of an upgrade is their 1776cc engine, which offers a great combination of power, useability and reliability. However, they say it is important for anyone looking to upgrade to choose the right ancillaries to complement the engine.

Whether going like-for-like, or upgrading, the options are limitless – but it is essential that the ancillaries are compatible, functioning and balanced to the new engine in respect of gaining optimal performance, reliability and longevity. For example, it is no use upgrading to a 1776cc with a bigger cam and then running a standard carburettor.

BOLT-ON UPGRADES

Exhaust

If there is nothing wrong with your engine – other than you would like a little more pep – you can buy a number of items off the peg to give it a helping hand. One of the first things a lot of people reach for is an after-market exhaust. An exhaust with a larger diameter helps the engine breathe better. This is because, when your engine is producing high rpm the gases are trying to escape, but are being restricted. A larger exhaust gives them more room to move about and reduces the back pressure in the system.

What exhaust you fit depends on a number of factors, namely price, looks and clearance. You will struggle to fit a

The CSP Python exhaust has been designed with perfectly matched pipe lengths for optimum flow patterns and maximum gas velocity.

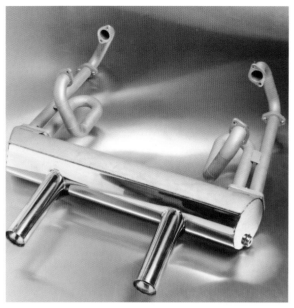

Stainless steel Vintage Speed exhaust has integrated tips and has been designed to fit like a standard VW system.

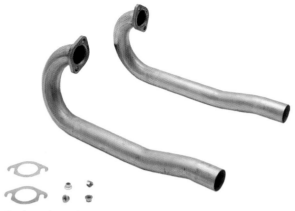

Fit a larger-bore exhaust and you may have to replace the heat exchangers (and lose the factory heating) with J-tubes. These ones are from CSP.

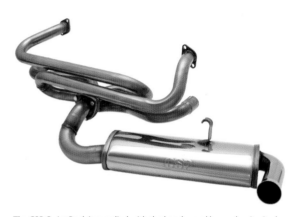

The CSP Quiet Pack is supplied with the header and has a classic, single muffler.

Abarth muffler has old-school looks and four tips that exit through the stock cut-outs in the valance for a fantastic sound, whatever size the engine.

big exhaust under the back of a really low Beetle, so something like a CSP Python is a fabulous addition to a high-performance engine but is best suited to a Cal Look car with its traditional nose down, rear in the air stance.

Twin carburettors

Replacing the stock single carb with dual carbs will give you an increase in horsepower and reduce fuel consumption if correctly jetted and set-up – assuming the driver has a light foot, that is. The fact is most people fit twin carburettors to boost power and drive with more gusto, so fuel economy actually goes down. Twin carbs alone won't be enough: if you are going to suck in more air, you need a better exhaust to let it out again.

Deep sump

Opinion is divided on these. If you run a low Volkswagen then you increase the risk of the bottom of the engine coming into contact with the ground and damaging the

Factory-style tail pipes give the CSP High-Flow exhaust a subtle look, but it sounds sporty and lasts, due to being made of stainless steel.

More air into an engine means more power. The way to do that is twin carbs.

sump. If you damage the sump and lose the engine oil, you could find yourself stranded miles from anywhere. The other school of thought is that the more oil you can have in your engine the cooler it will run and the happier it will be. A deep sump also reduces the risk of oil starvation as a result of enthusiastic driving, which is why a lot of performance VW engines have them fitted.

Vintage speed

Vintage speed is a term you will often hear bandied around the VW scene. It refers to old-school tuning methods and components that were *de rigueur* in the 1950s and '60s. Original Okrasa kits cost big money, but they're now being

reproduced and are a popular upgrade for those looking for a little more pep but who also want their engine to look period-correct.

An Okrasa kit is basically a pair of heads that turn a single-port engine into a dual port and it comes with a dual carb kit.

For the full Okrasa power upgrade you can buy an Okrasa crank, but that will require a full engine strip.

Speedwell/Pepco and Judson Superchargers are cool vintage speed modifications as well, but none of these will give you the same bang for your buck as say, a freshly built 1776cc. That said, you don't go down the vintage speed route if your only concern is speed – it's about the look and bragging rights, too.

Oil is the lifeblood of an air-cooled flat four; the more you have in it, the cooler it will run.

Original Okrasa kit and Abarth exhaust are period-perfect additions to this 30bhp Oval engine.

Transmission

7.1 Axle gaiters

Whilst the gearbox itself is a pretty robust unit, the same cannot be said of the rubber sleeves that wrap around the axle tubes on early swing-axle cars. Some later Beetles have Independent Rear Suspension (IRS) and Constant Velocity (CV) joints, which are something else entirely, but the majority of Beetles you will come across are equipped with a swing-axle rear end and axle gaiters.

How do you know what you've got? Easy – a swing-axle car will have just one rubber boot on the side that goes into the gearbox. It acts as a seal between the axle and transmission side covers. It goes up and down along with

TOP: *If you own a Beetle, at some point you will have to replace the axle gaiters.*

the rear suspension, whilst doing the incredibly important job of keeping the oil in and the dirt out. Contrarily, a Beetle with an IRS rear end has a rubber boot at each end of the axle and a CV joint.

The swing axle set-up is the cheaper option, which is why VW applied it to the Beetle. Like anything made out of rubber, axle gaiters don't last forever. They become brittle with age and then split. Your driveway will tell you when this has happened as there will be an oily mess wherever you park.

Fortunately, replacement gaiters are cheap and the job itself is not especially difficult. The worst part is simply getting to them and working comfortably. Popping a wheel off helps, but if you do that, be sure to support the car securely on axle stands.

A COMMON PROBLEM

This is a sight most Beetle owners will already be familiar with: the rubber of the gaiters becoming brittle with age, combined with the up and down movement of the rear axle eventually results in a split boot.

These aren't the factory originals, which are rare to find these days anyway. You will know if yours are original to the car if they are a single piece boot without a join in the middle. That's because in the factory they were slid onto the axle tube during assembly. Modern replacements have a join in the middle, so you don't have to remove the entire rear end to change them.

Incorrect orientation and split. Not good.

REMOVING THE OLD GAITER

This couldn't be any easier, although getting your hand and tool into position can be a little fiddly. There are six screws along the seam that need to come out and a hose clamp at either end to undo.

2. A snug-fitting screwdriver will have the Jubilee clips off in a jiffy.

Keep it clean

Have an old piece of rag, some blue roll or a drip tray handy to catch any oil that comes out. Then, give everything a good clean. You don't want to get any dirt in your new axle gaiter.

1. Use a 7mm socket or spanner to stop the rear nuts from spinning.

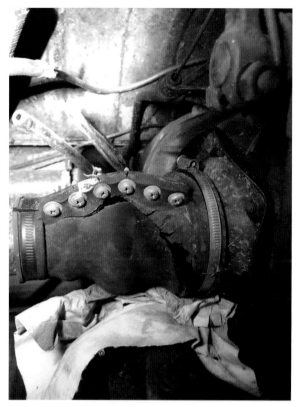

3. Old gearbox oil is particularly dirty and smelly, so be sure to wear gloves and old clothes for this particular task.

4. Place a tub underneath the axle and have plenty of cloths or blue roll handy to catch the oil that will inevitably trickle out.

REPLACEMENT PARTS

Remember what was said earlier about older parts normally being better than modern ones? Replacement gaiters are moulded with an integral seal. They slot together in one position and then you fasten them together. The issue here wasn't with the gaiter but with the nuts and screws that came with the kit. The new ones were tiny and didn't inspire much confidence, so instead the older, larger and more robust fittings that had been removed from the old gaiters were cleaned up and re-used.

5. Replacement gaiters have a serrated moulding that allows them to slot together in only one way.

6. Always compare new parts against old, just to be sure you have the right bits for the job at hand.

Installation

Slide your new gaiters into position and then start all of the hardware off by hand. Then, switch to using a snug, tight-fitting screwdriver. You need a 7mm spanner on the back of the boot screws and an 8mm helps snug the clamps down. Don't go too mad or you will distort the boot.

7. Start the Jubilee clips off with a screwdriver.

8. Snug the Jubilee clips up with an 8mm spanner.

9. Tighten the screws and, once the car is back on the ground, double-check the tightness of all fastenings.

Seams legit

VW recommends having the axle in the loaded/level position, but setting the car on an axle stand at just the right height does the trick.

There is some debate about the correct orientation for the seam. All of the cars the author has ever owned have had the seam running along the top of the axle, as those on the featured car were at the start of this job. However, according to an official VW workshop manual, the seam should be positioned horizontally and facing towards the back of the car.

Finally...

Don't forget to top up the gearbox oil. Remove the drain plug in the side of the transmission and top up until the oil begins to trickle out again. Job done.

10. Seam position is a hot potato. Ask five different people and you will get five different answers.

11. VW says this job should be carried out with the axles level. Setting an axle stand at the correct height does the trick.

12. If your gaiters have been split for a while there is every chance the oil will be low in the gearbox. Top it up with fresh gearbox oil.

7.2 Gearbox removal

The only maintenance a Bug's gearbox ever needs is confined to simply topping up or changing the oil (*refer* back to Chapter 5 on servicing for that). Faults are few, but a Bug's box will need replacing if you have one that is totally locked up, making some serious grumbling or whining sounds, or which frequently jumps out of gear.

A bit of transmission whine is acceptable, especially on an older car, but should you need a replacement gearbox, you ought to be able to pick up a decent used one cheaply enough or have your existing gearbox rebuilt. It is always recommended to have a gearbox rebuilt by someone who knows what they are doing, rather than attempting to tackle it yourself. It's one of those jobs that requires specialist tools and knowledge.

There are two types of Beetle rear ends – swing axle and IRS. All early Bugs have swing axles and later models, like

TOP: *This is a swing-axle gearbox. IRS 'boxes have constant-velocity joints at either end of the axles.*

the 1302 and 1303 Beetles, came with IRS (Independent Rear Suspension) with double-jointed drive-shafts.

Those double-jointed driveshafts make life a little easier for the would-be gearbox remover, as you can simply unbolt the CV joints from the gearbox sides and pull the gearbox out. With a swing-axle car, the gearbox comes out with the transaxles still attached, once you've unbolted them from the axle housings behind the brake backing plates.

For the benefit of this chapter we will concentrate on the more commonly seen swing-axle set-up.

To remove the gearbox, the engine needs also needs to come out, so we will assume that is already out of the way and crack on.

STRIPPING

Shifter coupling

The first job on the tick list is actually inside the car – under the rear seat, to be precise. Tilt the seat base back and you

1. This image shows the position of the coupling in relation to the gearbox, which is a swing-axle 'box.

2. Remove the three bolts and the axles will pull free of the spring plates.

will find an inspection hatch in the tunnel. Remove the retaining screw and pop the cover off. There should be a safety wire running through the square-headed bolts. Remove/cut this off and remove the bolt to separate the shift rod from the gearbox.

Axle housings

Remove the three retaining bolts that attach the axle housings to the rear spring plates. Or, if you're working on an IRS car, remove the Allen-head bolts from the CV joints so you can pull the drive shafts clear of the gearbox.

Front mount

There are two 17mm nuts attaching the gearbox front mount to the chassis. Remove these, the washers and the bolt for the earth strap.

Carrier bolts

The only thing holding the gearbox in place now should be the two hefty carrier bolts passing through the U-shaped carrier bracket. You will need a 27mm socket or spanner to remove them and then the gearbox is ready to come out.

4. This picture clearly shows the 27mm carrier bolts just below the rubber gearbox mounts.

5. The gearbox is mounted to the two rear frame horns on the chassis.

You can do this yourself with a trolley jack or enlist a friend to lend some muscle. The gearbox itself isn't too heavy but it's a little unwieldy, especially with the axles still attached if you're working on a swing-axle car.

FURTHER STRIPPING

If you are planning to replace the gearbox you will need to swap over the axles. Start by removing the axle gaiters and then the gearbox side plates. They're held in place by six nuts and you need to keep the side plates square, so use a soft-faced mallet if you need to persuade them to come off.

3. There are two studs in the chassis that bolt through the gearbox front mount and you can clearly see the holes for them here.

6. *The axle shaft is sandwiched between two fulcrum plates and held in place by a circlip and thrust washer.*

8. *An axle shaft, removed from its housing. Not much to it, is there?*

7. *A complete swing-axle transmission. Stripped and ready to be cleaned up prior to refitting.*

Behind the side plate you'll find a large O-ring, a large round plastic packing disc and some paper gaskets.

To remove the axle shaft, there is a stout snap-ring/circlip. Once that's out of the way you can remove the thrust washer that holds the axle-shaft in place, sandwiched between two fulcrum plates. It all makes sense when you're looking at it in the real world.

REASSEMBLY

Putting it all back together is just the opposite of the process you have just read. The only difficulty is keeping the fulcrum plates in position, as they like to slip out. A second pair of hands helps, especially whilst you're trying to get the circlip in. You can and should buy a complete axle tube gasket kit to ensure nothing leaks and everything goes back together with the correct tolerances. These kits come with a number of side-plate gaskets, the reason being they're not just gaskets, but shims that set the tolerance between the axle tube and plastic packing disc. Every car is potentially

9. *Setting the gasket thickness is a case of trial and error. Add or subtract until it feels right.*

different, so you will need to experiment with the gaskets before you have the right tolerances.

The axle tube needs to be able to move up and down freely with minimal end play (movement in and out). Getting this right is a case of trial and error, as you will have to tighten the side-plate retainer nuts down. They need to be tightened to 14ft lb with a torque wrench. Assuming you have got everything set correctly, it was all spotlessly clean before you started and the endplates weren't bent out of shape, there should be no leaks or need for any type of sealant. Some people recommend using it, but VW didn't use any from the factory; the gaskets alone should set the tolerances and prevent leakage.

Nose cone

You may need to switch the nose cone over if you're swapping one gearbox for another. Compare your new one against your original one and swap them over if necessary, using a new gasket. One thing you absolutely must do here is to ensure the gearbox is in neutral. You will know it is when all three forks line up so the hockey stick can go to any of them. There is nothing worse than assembling everything and then discovering you can't select all of the gears.

Gearbox mounts

If you have got the engine out you should take a moment to examine the condition of the rubber gearbox mounts. There is one at the front and two at the back and all are simple bolt-in items. These split over time and cost less than £10 for the front and about £20 for the two rears. You may as well change them now whilst you can get to them easily.

10. Always use new gaskets as you don't want to find a leak once everything is all put back together.

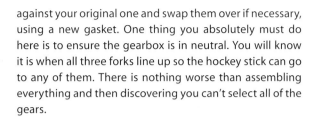

12. These are stock, rubber rear gearbox mounts.

13. Performance options would be urethane or even solid gearbox mounts, but the latter are not ideal for street use.

11. Bolted back together and with the front mounting points clearly visible.

7.3 Clutch and flywheel

These two components are lumped together because VW did the same on all of its air-cooled engines. You can't get to the flywheel oil seal without first removing the clutch and one of the main symptoms of a leaking flywheel oil seal is a clutch that slips under load. Oh, and usually a major oil leak coming from the bell-housing.

This isn't a particularly challenging job and the only specialist tools you actually need are: clutch alignment tools, which are cheap and sometimes included in the replacement clutch kit; a flywheel locking tool; a torque wrench – which you should already have, as you need one for lots of other jobs on your Beetle; and a long breaker bar.

Obviously, the engine will have to be removed to carry out this procedure, so refer back to the chapter on removal (Chapter 6.2) and then come back here.

A MAJOR LEAK

With the engine removed, this is the kind of sight you can expect to be faced with. A lot of VW owners joke about having a self-changing oil when they have a kippered flywheel oil seal – and you can see why. Your engine will use oil faster than petrol, so it really isn't one of those jobs you can ignore. Flywheel oil seals often fail after a car has been left sitting idle for a long time; the action of the engine spinning against the dried-out seal tears it and then leaks are inevitable.

TOP: *(left) The problem. A leak like this means it's time for a new flywheel oil seal.*
TOP: *(right) The cure. Flywheel oil seals are around £5 each. You can buy rubber seals or ones made from silicone, like this one.*

1. *Check the condition of the clutch release bearing. Now is the ideal time to change it.*

Remove clutch

There are a couple of different styles of clutch pressure plates, but they are all bolted to the flywheel in the same way. Remove the six 14mm bolts and washers and set them to one side. With the pressure plate removed the clutch disc will simply fall out. If your disc still has plenty of meat on the bone you can clean it up and reuse it, but they're usually so contaminated with oil and glazed from

2. The clutch pressure plate is bolted to the flywheel with six 14mm bolts. Remove them to remove the pressure plate.

3. This clutch is in surprisingly good condition and uses original VW parts. Reuse or replace?

4. If the friction surface isn't warped or damaged, you can clean it up and reuse it, but it's sensible to fit a new one at this point.

5. You will need to lock the flywheel in place to stop it spinning. The correct tool costs about £10.

slipping that you really are better off replacing them. Plus, for a little expense now, you will have peace of mind knowing that you won't be pulling the engine out again any time soon to replace the clutch. Do the job right and do it once.

Remove flywheel

The flywheel is bolted to the end of the crankshaft with a 36mm gland nut. You'll need to lock the flywheel into place to stop it from spinning. Fortunately, there's a spe-

8. The root cause of all this mess and work – a £5 part.

Remove old seal

The old flywheel oil seal can now be pried out of the engine case. Take a little care with this, as you don't want to gouge the engine casing. Also, make a mental note, or take a picture as a reference tool, so you remember how far your old seal sat in the engine. Some are inserted as far as they can go, others sit flush with the case. If you look online you will see a lot of people say the seal shouldn't be flush with the case, but always sit inside by a fraction or two at least. They argue that the seal rides too high on the collar of the flywheel if it's flush with the case and will be torn up as soon as you start the engine. The best solution is to replicate exactly what you removed. If the old one had been in there a long time the new one will hopefully last as long if it's installed the same way. Some have shims and a paper gasket, so be sure to put everything back in the correct order it came out, which will also ensure the new seal is fitted at the right depth.

Clean up

This flywheel was full of crud and old engine oil. Spend a few minutes cleaning yours out and checking it for any signs of wear or damage. Pay particular attention to the shoulder contact surface. If it has deep grooves in it, you will need to replace the flywheel. Don't forget to degrease

9. Clean up the flywheel. Ensure the snout is particularly clean or you risk damaging the new seal on start up.

6. A length of scaffold tube over your breaker bar can provide the leverage you need to crack the gland nut off.

7. With the gland nut removed, the flywheel can now be wiggled or carefully pried off.

cific tool for this job and it only costs a few pounds. Locate it on the flywheel teeth and fasten the bolt to tighten it down. The gland nut is torqued to 220ft lb, so can be a swine to remove. If you begged/borrowed/bought a 'Mr Torque' tool for working on your rear hub nuts, the good news is it also works on flywheel gland nuts. If not, it's time to reach for a hefty breaker bar. Sliding an old piece of scaffold tube over the top of this usually provides the kind of leverage you need. Before you do, however, it's a good idea to make some alignment marks on the flywheel and engine case; that way you know it should all go back together the same way and still be in balance. You can also do this on the gland nut to give you a visual clue to the torque setting.

10. *Remove all traces of oil from the engine to prevent it contaminating the new clutch.*

11. *Using the correct tool ensures the new seal goes in squarely.*

the engine case and gearbox bell-housing. You don't want to contaminate your new clutch, do you?

INSTALL THE NEW SEAL

Ensure the seal recess is clean and fit the new seal. Some people like to apply a thin smear of sealing adhesive, others say the new seal should go in dry. The side with the spiral spring on view must face inside the engine and the seal itself must go in straight. There is a special tool you can buy that winds it in squarely, but it costs nearly £50, so most people start it off with their fingers and then tap it home a bit at a time around the rim. However, the best way to install it correctly without the tool is to place a piece of wood over

it and hit that instead. That way, it should go in straight and you reduce the chance of damaging the face of the seal.

O-ring

Prior to the introduction of the 1300cc engine of 1966, all flywheels featured a paper gasket that fitted between the crankshaft and flywheel. It was dropped in favour of an O-ring that slotted inside the flywheel hub. Hook your old one out, clean out the groove and install the new O-ring. Some people like to lubricate it with oil, others apply a little silicone sealant to it before bolting the flywheel on – but if you do that you will need to fit the flywheel before it's had the chance to set.

12. *Don't forget the O-ring or paper gasket, depending on the year of car.*

13. Performance engines have eight dowls; a standard crank makes do with only four.

14. A little lubrication can make the difference between a job well-done and the need for round two.

Dowel pins

A stock engine will have four dowels protruding from the end of the crank. They locate and keep the flywheel in place on the crank. Don't panic if one falls out: they're not fixed into place, but saying that, they should be a snug fit. Examine them for signs of wear or damage. If a flywheel comes loose due to being incorrectly torqued, it can damage the dowels and round out the locating holes.

Lubrication

Use some fresh oil to lubricate the contact surface and inner lip of the new oil seal and the snout of the flywheel itself. If you don't you run the risk of it tearing due to friction.

Gland nut

Refit the gland nut and tighten. You will need your 36mm socket, a large breaker bar and torque wrench. Many people simply stand on the end of the breaker bar and tighten it as much as they can, but you really don't want to over-tighten and break the gland nut. You can use a Mr Torque to multiply the torque and make life a little easier for yourself, but the gland nut needs to be torqued to 217ft lb for 1200cc, 1300cc and 1500cc engines and 253ft lb for 1600cc/IRS cars.

15. A little bit tighter than spec is all right; a little bit looser can be really, really bad.

Install the clutch

Use a clutch alignment tool to align the friction plate in the splines and bolt the pressure plate back on. Work your way around the pressure plate, taking your time as you tighten to avoid distorting it. Torque the bolts to 20ft lb and if you want, a little Loctite glue to secure things further is a good idea.

16. A clutch alignment tool won't break the bank and is absolutely vital for this job.

18. A new clutch was on its way, so the old one was fitted for the benefit of these pictures.

17. With the pressure plate installed.

7.4 Shift rod

Have you ever wondered what the little round access panel in a Beetle's front valance is for? The comedians out there like to say it's where the starting handle used to go, but it's actually there so that you can remove the shift rod from the transmission tunnel. Whilst that's not a job you need to do very often, you might if you have issues with selecting gears and it's not the fault of the gearbox, clutch or clutch cable.

There is a little plastic bush in the tunnel under the gear lever and when it wears you end up with a sloppy shift. It sits in a round metal guide that is welded to the inside of the transmission tunnel. The guide contains the two captive nuts that the gear lever bolts into. In extreme cases these need to be replaced. The good news is that they are cheap to replace; the downside is you will have to cut a hole in the transmission tunnel to do so. Fortunately, if you only need to replace the plastic bushing, you can do this by removing the gear lever and applying a little manual dexterity.

GEAR SHIFTER

This little blighter can be the cause of a great many shifting issues. There is a metal stop plate below the lever and

1. Remove or pull the tunnel carpet back to avoid getting grease on it. Note how the shifter is arranged to the left, in order to best suit left-hand-drive cars.

TOP: *(left) A handy cut-away showing how the gear lever attaches to the shift rod.*
TOP: *(right) You can clearly see the guide tube for the shift rod in this photo. This is where the new bushing goes.*

the entire assembly needs to be bolted down in exactly the right position. A little too much either to the left or the right and you'll struggle getting the car into gear or it will pop out when you are driving. Yours might be out of alignment

2. If your shift boot is split like this, replace it to prevent dirt getting in.

3. Make a note of which way the shifter plate goes on.

if someone has removed the lever to grease the ball-end or maybe done some interior work, like changing the carpet over the tunnel. Whatever the state of play, the stop plate needs to be correctly aligned and the assembly tightened down to hold it all in place. Mark the position of yours with tape or scribe a line if you want everything to go back exactly the same way it came out.

The shift lever is held in place by two 14mm bolts. Remove them and the lever should pop out of the chassis spine, as there is a large spring underneath. Take note of how it sits on the stop plate and which way round the plate sits – the raised lip goes on the right-hand side.

ACCESS PANELS

Open the front trunk/frunk/boot – whatever you like to call it – and remove the spare wheel. There should be a little round access panel held in place with a metal tang and screw. Remove it and the one in the front valance if you have a post-'67 car with a short bonnet. Early cars just have a cut-out under the latch mechanism, but later cars have a removable plate. Also, it's not unheard of for some people to delete these little access panels for a cleaner look when replacing the spare wheel well and front valance. Should this be the case, you're in for a lot more work.

4. VW included these factory access panels for a reason. Locate and remove the first one in the spare wheel well.

5. A metal tang and one screw hold it in place.

6. Later cars, with shorter bonnets, have an access panel in the front valance; earlier cars have a simple hole you can't see with the bonnet closed.

7. There is another access panel in the frame head. This has to come off so you can pull the shift-rod out of the chassis.

There is another access panel in the chassis spine. You will find this under the car, between the two front axle tubes. Undo the two retaining bolts and pop it off.

Shift rod coupling

There is another access panel under the rear seat. You will have to cut/remove the locking wire from the front screw of the coupling and then you should be able to pull the shift rod forward and out of the car. Wear gloves, as it's usually pretty filthy down there.

Shift rod guide

If yours has given up the ghost – the metal ring section can break – you will have to cut a hole in the chassis spine to get to it. To fix a new guide in place you can drill holes in the spine, bolt the new piece into place and then weld it in as shown.

8. Wear gloves, as it's a pretty filthy job removing a shift-rod.

9. The most difficult part of this repair is getting in to do it.

10. *This job is much easier when you can do it by sight, rather than just feel.*

11. *Lining up the shift plate with the stop positioned on the correct side.*

Shift rod bushing

The plastic bush simply slots into place. It has a wire ring to help reduce shift rod noise and hold it together. Once in place, grease up the shift rod, slide it back through the access holes and reattach the coupling.

GREASE UP AND REFIT

Apply fresh grease to the gear lever ball housing. Ensuring everything is clean and well lubricated is a great way to stave off the need for future work. Reinstall the stop plate, spring and gear lever and ensure you can select all forward and reverse gears without the lever popping out when the car is in motion. If everything is correctly aligned you should be all set for trouble-free shifting.

12. *Stick a good blob of grease on the shifter ball and in the socket for lubrication.*

13. *Lubricated, fitted and like nothing ever happened.*

7.5 Troubleshooting

Many people new to the world of VW Beetles often express difficulties with the gears. The long throw of the gear lever, the long, spindly lever itself and just the general vagueness of selecting the right gear are common gripes.

If you have never driven a perfectly set-up Beetle before, you may incorrectly assume that all Beetles are like that, or there is something seriously wrong with the gearbox. Neither of which is usually the case. Something as simple as an incorrectly set-up gear lever can make finding the right gear a living hell.

You change gears in a Beetle using a bunch of mechanical levers, rods and cables. If any of them are worn, damaged or out of alignment, you are going to run into difficulties. The trick is working out which part of the system you need to fix.

As has already been stated, Beetle gearboxes are pretty tough little units, so there is actually not an awful lot to go wrong.

Most problems can be traced to the lever, the cable or the clutch itself. For example, if your clutch slips, grabs, jerks or makes a weird noise and adjusting the cable doesn't fix it, it's the clutch that is at fault. Which means the engine has to come out to fix it. Hence, it is always recommended to look at the simple stuff first. If all of the easy bits to check work out, it is time to dig a little deeper, but what are the issues you may encounter?

TOP: *This excellent training chassis perfectly illustrates how the Beetle's gearbox works.*

TROUBLESHOOTING GUIDE FOR WHEN THE CAR WON'T GO INTO GEAR

Difficulty selecting gears
1. Gear lever is out of alignment.
2. Clutch cable needs adjusting.
3. Transmission fluid low or wrong viscosity.
4. Bent or worn synchro mechanism.
5. Faulty clutch or clutch release bearing.

Crunching gears
1. Gear lever is out of alignment.
2. Clutch cable needs adjusting.
3. Transmission fluid low or wrong viscosity.
4. Bent or worn synchro mechanism.
5. Faulty clutch or clutch release bearing.
6. Worn out clutch.

Noisy gearbox (in neutral)
1. Transmission fluid low or wrong viscosity.
2. Worn bearings/bushes.
3. Main drive shaft has excessive end float.

Noisy gearbox (in gear)
1. Gearbox low on oil.
2. Worn drive and pinion shaft bearings.
3. Worn reverse idler gear.

Jumping out of gear
1. Gear lever is out of alignment.
2. Worn gearshift mechanism.
3. Selector fork out of alignment.
4. Worn bearings.
5. Worn gear or pinion shaft.

Dragging clutch
1. Too much slack in clutch cable, cable needs adjusting.

Slipping clutch
1. Oil contamination from a leak.
2. Clutch cable needs adjusting.

Oil leaks
1. Split axle gaiters.
2. Worn rear transmission seal.
3. Loose side-cover nuts.
4. Damaged joint washers/joint faces.
5. Worn gear shift bushes.

7.6 Modifications/upgrades

Truth be told, there is not a huge amount you can do to improve a Beetle's gearbox and shifting. At least, not within the budget of most people, anyway. If you have the money to spend, you can buy a five-speed gearbox from the likes of Gene Berg or Bears Motorsport, but they're really more for drag racing. The Berg, for example, provides an extra gear between third and fourth to get you down the track faster. Either company will build you a gearbox to your requirements, but truth be told, most Beetle owners simply put up with four speeds and regular downshifts on hills.

There are a number of UK parts specialists who can supply you with a new gearbox from Rancho Performance Transaxles in either swing axle or IRS set-ups, but the vast majority of people, when or if they need to source a replacement gearbox, head to the swap meets and buy what they hope is a decent like-for-like replacement.

If you want more relaxed cruising on long journeys and you don't want to spend a fortune, your best option is to

TOP: *Few things improve the feel of a Beetle as much as an aftermarket gear lever and steering wheel.*

track down an original gearbox from a 1500cc or 1600cc (GT) Beetle. GT Editions and 1303S Beetles have a higher gear ratio with a taller fourth gear than a standard 1200cc or 1300cc Beetle.

To make the most of what is really not such a bad thing, once you have got used to it, you are best off ensuring that there is plenty of oil in the gearbox, the shifter is perfectly adjusted and there is no slop in the shift rod, all of which topics have been covered elsewhere in this book.

If you want to improve the feel of the gearshift – by making it more positive and reducing the amount of throw in the lever – you can do that easily enough with an after-market gear lever, and there are seemingly countless options available to you.

Over the years, the author has come to realize that you cannot go wrong with anything from CSP (www.csp-shop.com). Custom & Speed Parts, to give them their full name, are a German company who manufacture and ship top quality parts all over the world. They are often a little more expensive than other options, but they're built to last, designed to fit properly and adhere to strict German standards.

Let's consider a few of the options.

A Rancho Performance gearbox is a good option for anyone looking for a new replacement 'box.

Quick shift kit

The CSP quick shift kit is by far the cheapest and best-looking option for the Beetle owner who wants their car to look factory original.

The quick shift plate mounts beneath your stock shifter base and reduces the amount of throw in the lever by a good 30 to 40 per cent, giving you a more positive feel and much faster shift.

Locking shifter

This won't improve the feel, but it will reduce the chances of your car being stolen. This is a modern reproduction of

A reproduction Sperrwolf shifter is available from a variety of suppliers; this one came from Machine7.

the Sperr Wolf locking gear shifter that was available back in the day. It locks the car into neutral so no one can drive it away. Vintage looks and practical too.

CSP T-handle

A quality piece of kit made using CNC-milled aluminium. The T-handle feels nice in your hand and the shifter throw is reduced by 40 per cent over standard. You can also buy a rapid shift version that reduces it by 60 per cent. The push button is for selecting reverse and all CSP shifters come with a new reverse lock-out plate, bolts and full assembly instructions.

The CSP T-handle is the same length as a stock Beetle shifter, but that's the only similarity.

If you love the look of a stock shifter, a CSP quick shift kit is the way to go.

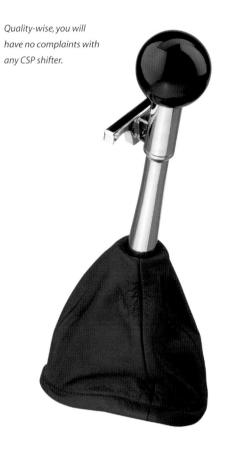

Quality-wise, you will have no complaints with any CSP shifter.

The absolute king of the after-market Beetle gear shifter world goes by the name of Gene Berg.

CSP ball-handle

The same quality and functionality of the T-handle, but with a non-reflective black gear knob. Reverse is accessed by means of the butterfly trigger on the front of the lever, which can be ordered as a straight or bent bar, like the T-handle version. It's just a case of which style you prefer.

Gene Berg

We can't talk about after-market VW shifters without mentioning Gene Berg. These legendary offerings were made for the original Cal Look cars back in the day and are still being produced today. They are available with a variety of throws, handle styles and in locking and non-locking format.

EMPI Hurst

EMPI made hundreds of aftermarket parts for Beetles back in the day and one of the most popular was their take on the Hurst-style shifter. They are still incredibly popular today and don't cost a fortune when bought from the likes of Machine7 (www.machine7.com), making them the perfect mix of both affordability and function. The lockout trigger on the front prevents you from accidentally grabbing reverse when banging through the gears and they have a nice, positive feel to them.

Vintage Speed

Not a cheap option, but quality never is. The author ran one of these in a Camper for years and had zero issues with it. They are a mix of old-school and modern race-inspired looks and come in a variety of styles and colours, again from the likes of Machine7.

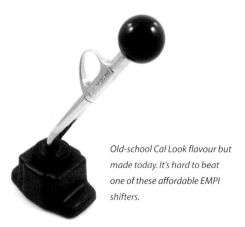

Old-school Cal Look flavour but made today. It's hard to beat one of these affordable EMPI shifters.

Looks are subjective, so buy whichever shifter you like and can afford. These are all great upgrades, but this one is from Vintage Speed.

Brakes and Bearings

8.1 Front brakes

Brakes are without a doubt the single most important components on your car. Any faults in the braking system should be rectified immediately and the car should not be driven until whatever repairs deemed necessary have been carried out. There are number of things that can and do go wrong with the Beetle's braking system, but they are easy to work on and replacement parts are both cheap and plentiful.

TOP: *This is a stock, early Beetle front drum brake – but they are all pretty similar.*

The vast majority of Beetles were built with drum brakes all round, but '67 1500s, Mexican Beetles and a few other special editions came with discs on the front and drums on the back. The car pictured here is an early model and has what are known as five-bolt drums all round. They are called 'five-bolt' because the wheels are attached to the car with five bolts and have a 5 × 205 bolt pattern. Later '68-onwards cars are known as four-bolt cars for obvious reasons and come with the 4 × 130 bolt pattern.

WORKING ON YOUR BEETLE'S BRAKES

The extra hole in the front of the drum shown on the previous page is for adjusting the shoes, but later cars have the inspection hole in the backing plate. The hole in the front makes it easier to see the star adjusters but harder to adjust as the drum moves about whilst you're adjusting them.

If you need to replace your Beetle's brake shoes you should never just replace one side; you should always replace both sides to ensure there is the same amount of lining material side to side.

Speedo cable

You'll need to remove the speedo cable. It's routed through the back of the drum through the spindle in the front near-side wheel and is secured via a circlip. Remove the circlip and pull the cable through from the back of the drum.

Spindle nuts, lock tabs and washers

To remove the drum, pry off the dust cover to reveal the spindle nuts. Early cars have a lock washer tapped around 27mm spindle nuts to prevent them working loose. Later cars/modified examples have a locking nut tightened via an Allen key. Bend the locking tab back, loosen the Allen bolt and then remove the spindle nuts. VW spindle nuts are handed, that is the left-hand spindle has a left-hand thread and right spindle has a right-hand thread. The thinking behind this is that the spindle nuts won't work loose as the car moves forward.

2. Behind the nuts you will find a large, flat washer.

3. Remove the washer.

Outer bearings

If you are planning to re-use your bearings, be extra careful not to drop them as dirt and wheel bearings are not a good combination. Pop them into a zip-lock bag or a clean storage container and then clean and repack the bearing with fresh grease when you come to reinstall them.

1. Don't lose the circlip, as without it your speedo cable will slide back through the hole and not function properly.

4. This old-style roller bearing had been in the car for some time.

6. Remove three bolts and the brake hose and backing plate will come straight off.

Remove drum

You will most likely need to back the shoes off to get the drum to clear the inner lip. Pop one of the spindle nuts back on and give it a yank. If it comes free it will only come as far as the spindle nut and not smack you in the face.

5. Sometimes a few taps with a mallet are required to get the get the drum off.

The brakes on the featured car were in pretty good shape and the linings had enough meat left on them so didn't need replacing just yet. Leaking cylinders are a common issue and brake fluid can saturate the shoe and render the brake useless.

Strip down

You can strip drums in situ but in this case the plan was to change the front beam, so everything had to come off anyway. The backing plate is held to the spindle by three 17mm bolts and you will also have to release the brake hose from the back of the drum if you're removing it or just changing the cylinder. Have something to catch any fluid that escapes.

Springs and washers

With the drum assembly on a work bench, begin by removing the shoe locating springs and washers. A pair of pliers, a bit of pressure and a twist of the wrist does the trick.

Wheel cylinder

The shoe return springs will now come free and you can remove those and the shoes from the backing plate. The wheel cylinder is bolted to the backing plate by a single 13mm bolt. Remove the bolt and the cylinder should simply pop out.

7. Clean and reuse these, as modern replacements tend to be of poor quality.

8. The cylinders were in reasonable condition, but it was decided to replace them anyway.

Adjusting screws

Wind out the brake adjusting screws. These should be nice and loose in the star adjusters, but those on the featured car were well and truly gummed up and meant there was no way to adjust the front brakes at all.

Star adjusters

The star adjusters were equally seized, which explains why it was impossible to get them to turn in either direction when an attempt at adjusting the brakes was made. They were stuck fast in the anchor block.

9. These should turn freely.

10. With the backing plate held in the vice, a good tap with a screwdriver set them free.

12. Always paint in a well-ventilated area and follow the manufacturer's instructions.

Free up

Now's the time to ensure everything works as it should. As the brake adjusters were seized solid, a small wire brush on the end of a drill was used to remove any dirt and rust from the anchor block.

11. Be sure to wear gloves and eye protection when using a wire wheel on a drill.

Clean up

Now you could just fit any new components where necessary, or take the opportunity to clean off all the old dirt and rust and paint the drum and backing plate. It makes reassembly so much nicer and your car look fresher. You can use a cheek poker (wire wheel) on a drill to remove the dirt and surface rust.

Budget resto

Obviously, you could have your backing plates blasted and powder coated to achieve a smoother and longer lasting finish, but the budget option is a rattle can in the garage, which is what was chosen here. The end result was good enough.

13. It is little jobs like this that make all the difference.

14. A pot of copper grease costs very little, but its true value can't be quantified.

Copper grease

If these items won't turn you can't adjust your brakes, so a liberal coating of copper grease should keep everything freed-up for years to come.

Reuse or replace?

Original parts are more often than not better quality than replacements. The shoe locating pins and washers are a prime example. The new ones are terrible, being cheap quality and entirely the wrong shape for the pins to locate in the washers.

On the bench

It's much easier to fit the locating pins on a bench than on the car, as you can place something on the rear to hold the pins in place whilst you turn the washers. These have a nasty habit of pinging across the garage if you're not careful.

Wise move

Everything cleaned up, fitted and the backing plate bolted back onto the spindle. The only component actually replaced was the cylinder and that wasn't strictly necessary, more a precaution, so the biggest investment here was time.

Spotlessly clean

Before you pop the drum back on, you need to ensure the shoes and the internal drum surfaces are clean. Grease and brake fluid will seriously compromise your car's braking ability, so use brake cleaner to remove any greasy finger prints or contamination and then give the shoe a scuff to roughen up the surface. However, one thing to note is that really old Beetles were equipped with asbestos brake linings. There are probably not that many cars still running them, but it is something to be aware off as you really don't want to breathe in asbestos.

15. Cleaned up, these ancient originals were a better fit than the new ones acquired.

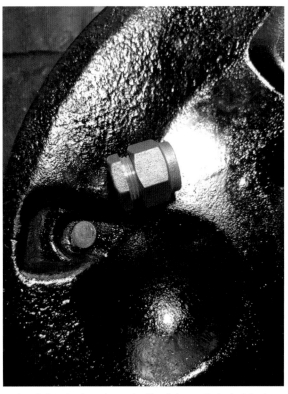

16. A well-placed socket or brass plumbing fitting on the back of the drum helps hold the pins in position.

17. Good as new.

Adjustment

All that remains is to adjust the shoes through the inspection hole in the drum. Most people use a screwdriver, but you can buy the correct adjusting tool for just a couple of pounds to make life easier. Nip inside the car and press the brake pedal to centre the shoes and then wind them out using the star adjusters.

Wind the shoes out until you can't move the drum anymore and then wind them back in so that it can spin again. You want to hear a light dragging noise and, when you do, they're correctly adjusted. Press the brake pedal again and recheck. Bolting the wheel back on can help with spinning the drum, but you can't get to the adjuster if you're running an after-market wheel.

Take your car for a test drive and ensure everything is working as it should. It can take a little time for new shoes to bed in, but if the car pulls to one side for example, then they're incorrectly adjusted.

Adjusting the rear brakes is exactly the same procedure as that for the fronts.

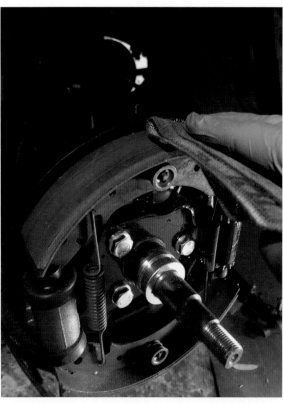

18. Use a piece of medium-grit sandpaper to roughen up the friction surface and remove any glazing from the shoe.

19. Early cars have an adjuster hole in the front of the drum; later Beetles have holes in the back of them.

8.2 Front wheel bearings

All Beetles, whatever the year or production, have wheel bearings. An ominous rumble whilst driving is a sure-fire sign that one of them is unhappy. Classic symptoms are a low growling or squealing sound that alters with the speed of the vehicle, and often disappears when turning a corner.

VW recommended servicing the wheel bearings every 48,280km (30,000 miles). Whilst it is possible to clean up an old bearing, repack it with fresh grease and retighten, replacement bearings are easy to fit and don't exactly cost the earth.

Each drum has two bearings, consisting of an inner bearing and race and an outer bearing and race.

Bearings and races are matched sets, so you can't use a new bearing in an old race. If you have to replace a bearing, you also have to fit a new race with it.

TOP: *Everything you need to replace the inner and outer wheel bearings on one front drum.*

CHANGING YOUR WHEEL BEARINGS

The previous chapter showed how to remove the front drum and now, with the drum transferred to the workbench, it is time to dive in and change the bearings.

Outer bearing

Once you've popped the dust cap off and removed the locking washers and lock nuts, the outer bearing should simply fall out when you pull the drum towards you.

Dust seal

The inner bearing has a dust seal. This needs to be pried out with a screwdriver and then thrown in the bin. Some people like to re-use the old seal, especially if it's an original VW piece, but all good bearing kits should come with a new one so it's good practice to use one you know wasn't damaged during removal.

This is an older-style roller bearing, but we replaced ours with the newer-style taper bearing.

Some replacement seals can be poor quality, so most owners reuse the genuine VW ones if they are able.

Bearing races

The inner and outer races need to be drifted out. A large screwdriver and hammer are the tools for this job, but go easy as you don't want to damage the drum whilst tapping them out. For the outer race you'll need to create a little room for the race to fall out of the end. Placing the drum in a vice or over two pieces of wood should give you the space you need.

1. Add some blocks of wood to your list of essential garage equipment.

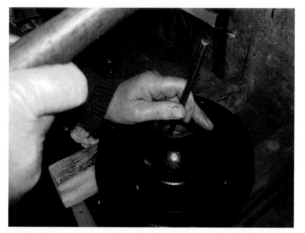

2. Place the drum over the blocks and tap the inner race out.

3. Flip the drum over and tap the outer race out. You need a bit of space for the bearing to be tapped all the way out, hence the blocks.

4. Brake cleaner and plenty of rags are essential ingredients for this task.

Clean surfaces

With both races removed you need to thoroughly clean up the centre of the drum to remove any traces of dirt and debris. You can then pack a third of the space between the races with fresh bearing grease, which will help ease the new ones into place.

Install new races

It is vitally important that the new races go in correctly. They need to slide in squarely or you risk destroying the new race and possibly damaging the mating surface in the drum. Don't tap your new races in with anything sharp like a screwdriver; use the correct tool for the job, which is a bearing driver. If you're using one of these then be sure to select the correct size. You don't want it to get stuck inside the drum. You need to drive the race home until it's fully seated, and you can tell this when the tone of the hammer changes.

Pack bearings with grease

You need to ensure the new bearings are fully packed with a suitable bearing grease. It's a messy job but essential if you want your bearings to be happy and last another 48,280km (30,000 miles).

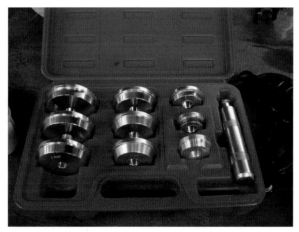

5. An 11-piece bearing driver set can be picked up for less than £20 online.

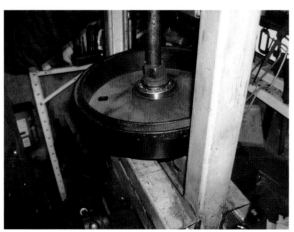

6. With access to a press, installing the new races is so much easier.

7. Grease up the new bearings.

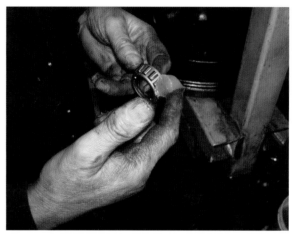

8. Don't be tempted to skimp on the grease. You need to ensure every surface has a good covering.

Install grease seal

With the inner bearing fully greased up and ready to go, it's time to fit the new grease seal. Again, it needs to go in squarely. Start it off by hand and then you can either place a piece of wood over the top and tap it in with a soft-faced mallet or use a press. Either way, you need to ensure the seal goes in straight and hasn't been damaged whilst fitting. It needs to sit flush with the outer surface of the hub.

9. Applying a little grease around the edge helps ease the way.

REFIT THE DRUM

You need to ensure there is absolutely no grease on the internal braking surfaces of the drum. Grab some brake cleaner and give everything a thorough going over. Once you are happy with it, apply a smear of grease to the spindle and then with the adjusters backed all the way off, slide the drum back onto the spindle.

If any grease tries to escape, you can push all that the hub will hold back into the drum and then fit the outer bearing to hold it in place.

Add the thrust washer and one of the spindle nuts and then snug it down with a 27mm spanner/socket whilst rotating the drum in the opposite direction. You don't want to go too heavy – around 15ft lb is plenty and this helps properly seat the bearing. The drum should bind up. When it does, slacken the spindle nut back off so that the drum spins freely again. Then, slowly retighten whilst spinning the drum in the opposite direction again. This takes the play out of the bearing.

You know the amount of play is right when you can just move the thrust washer with a little pressure from a flat-bladed screwdriver. You don't want to be prying or twisting it against the drum, just using the edge to get it to move. That initial movement gives the wheel the 0.001-inches to 0.005-inches of play that you're looking for. Too loose and the wheel will wobble, too tight and the bearing will run hot, cook the grease and ruin the bearing.

Add the lock nut and ensure both nuts are locked tightly together with the securing tab washer. Later models have an outer spindle nut with an Allen screw and no tab washer, but adjusting it is the same process.

Re-check the play in the thrust washer and then install the dust cap. You should pop some fresh grease inside this and then tap it home, pulling the speedo cable through and securing with a circlip. Refit the wheel and give it a spin by hand. The wheel should spin freely without any binding. If you hear any clunking or detect any play in the wheel it means something isn't right. Remember to adjust your brakes and then you should be good to go.

11. Installing the lock nut and locking tab.

10. When you can just move the thrust washer with the end of a screwdriver, the play is correct.

12. Check for play after a few miles and adjust if necessary.

8.3 Rear brakes, hubs and bearings

All Beetles left the factory equipped with rear drum brakes. Working on them is exactly the same process as with the fronts, the only difference being how you remove the drum.

The biggest stumbling block for most people working on the rear brakes is that the rear axle nuts that hold the drum in place are torqued to 217ft lb. The high torque means you don't have to worry about setting the free play, but getting them off can be an absolute beast of a job.

PREPARING THE WORK

It can be incredibly dangerous trying to remove the axle nuts with the vehicle supported on a jack/axle stand, so you should only attempt to remove them with the vehicle sitting on all four wheels. The trick is to apply the handbrake and if that's not enough, have someone sitting in the car with their foot firmly pressed on the brake pedal. A long cheater bar, like a piece of scaffold tube, can provide the extra leverage you need to break them loose.

TOP: *Drum brakes are essentially all the same. The only difficult part of working on the rears is getting the hub nuts off.*

The other alternative – and highly recommended – is to buy or ideally, borrow, a Mr Torque tool. These cost a little over £100 new, hence the suggestion that you borrow one from a VW friend if possible, but they make light work of rear hub nuts and flywheel gland nuts because they multiply the amount of leverage you apply from a normal ratchet, as you're about to see.

Hub nut

The rear hub nuts measure in at a hefty 36mm, so you will need a socket in that size. A sturdy breaker bar is an absolute must if you don't have a torque multiplier, but life is so much easier if you can beg, borrow or buy one. It bolts to the drum as shown and makes light work of even the most stubborn of hub nuts. There should be a split pin in the hub/castle nut, so remove that first and then remove the nut.

Remove drum

Release the handbrake and slacken off the brakes using the star adjusters and the drum should slip off the axle. It may need a little gentle persuasion with a soft-faced mallet, but

1. A Mr Torque tool makes removing rear hub nuts so much easier.

2. Rear hub nuts are also known as castle nuts, for obvious reasons, and are designed to be fitted with split pins.

3. A common sight when you remove any Beetle's drum.

it will come off eventually. A top tip here is to wind the hub nut back on a few threads. That way, when you yank the drum towards you, it will only come as far as the castle nut and not biff you in the face when it pulls free.

With the drum removed, the dog can see the rabbit. The linings on the featured car had plenty of meat left on them but were heavily contaminated with oil and brake fluid so needed replacing. Leaking cylinders are an all too common issue and brake fluid seeping through these will saturate the shoes and render the brake useless. The only thing to do is clean everything thoroughly and replace the cylinder.

Clean up

Stripping down a rear drum is exactly the same as working on the front, the only difference being the handbrake mechanism on the rears. With the drum and backing plate transferred to the bench, they were degreased and cleaned of all rust with a wire wheel on a drill. A few coats of paint and they were good enough. If the splines in the drum show any signs of wear, that means the hub nut has

4. Taking the budget clean-up route with a wire wheel on the end of a drill.

5. Painted with a coat of primer and left to dry. Always follow the manufacturer's instructions when painting.

6. Not show-car quality, but presentable – and should stand up nicely to the UK climate.

not been torqued to the correct spec. Some owners like to scribe a line on the castle nut and axle so they don't have to measure the torque during reassembly. This is all right if they were correctly torqued before you started.

Rear hub seals

In order to get the drum backing plate off you will have to remove the four 14mm rear hub nuts that hold it to the axle. There is a seal arrangement inside the square-shaped bearing cover that stops the oil in the axle tubes getting into the rear brakes. These are another common source of leaks and replacing them is pretty straightforward, at least once you have got the axle nut off. It can be a messy job, so ensure

you have plenty of rags to hand and some form of container to catch any oil that inevitably falls out.

Bearing cover

Once you have removed all of the old sealing components from the bearing cover, give it a thorough clean and then reassemble it with new parts. The first piece to go in is the washer, followed by the new seal. Rub a little oil around the seal to lubricate it and then push it in squarely with your fingers. It won't go in all the way, so place the old seal against it and tap it in the rest of the way with a soft-faced mallet. Don't hit it too hard. If you damage or distort the new seal you will have to buy another one.

7. An oil leak from the rear that is not coming from the brake cylinder is usually the result of a perished hub seal.

8. The back of the bearing cover, cleaned and ready to go.

9. The washer goes back in first.

10. Followed by the new rubber seal.

11. You can use a well-fitting socket as a drift, but take your time and don't damage the new seal.

12. No signs of damage. Perfect.

Once the seal is fully home, attach the big O-ring and paper gasket.

Rear wheel bearing

Now it's time to focus your attention on the rear axle. There's a metal spacer that goes on first, followed by the fully greased-up new bearing. A large O-ring goes around this, followed by an oil slinger metal washer and a small rubber O-ring gasket that slides over the axle splines.

13. The metal spacer is fitted first.

14. Pack the new bearing with plenty of fresh grease.

15. Don't forget the O-ring and now you are ready to bolt the cover back on.

16. Taking plenty of photos during removal helps with reassembly.

Torque it up

Slide the bearing cover on and bolt it through the brake backing cover to the rear axle. The 14mm bolts need to be torqued up to 43ft lb. With that done, you're ready to build the rear brakes back up again.

Brake components

Start by transferring the (clean) handbrake lever to the new shoes. They have a little button that passes through the

17. Always fit a new paper gasket, or fresh leaks will be sure to follow.

18. A torque wrench is essential for jobs like this. If you don't have one, buy one.

19. Transfer the handbrake mechanism over to the new shoes.

22. Locate the brake cylinder on the backing plate.

20. Fold the little tangs around to secure to the drum.

23. Bolt the cylinder down with a 13mm socket.

21. Lubricate with copper grease and reinstall the adjuster screws and star adjusters in the adjuster block.

24. Assemble the spreader bar, like so.

lever and into the shoe. It has a collar that you have to bend the retaining clip around to hold it in place but still allows it to move. Give the star adjusters a good coating of copper grease and slide them into the anchor block. Next, fasten the new cylinder in place from behind, using the 13mm bolt. Attach the shoe return spring to the handbrake push-rod and place the entire assembly on the backing plate. Install the two shoe locating springs and washers and pull the handbrake cable through the drum. Then attach it to the bottom of the lever.

25. Attach the shoes to the backing plate. Cheap repro cup washers and pins can be an absolute pain to fit.

27. Assembled. There's not much to it really.

Refit drum

Slide the drum back onto the splined axle, fit the castle/hub nut and tighten it up as best you can. Then, remove the car from the axle stands and lower it to the ground in order to tighten the castle nut to 217ft lb with a torque wrench. A little more than 217ft lb is okay, but any less is not acceptable. The space in the castellations and holes in the axle have been designed to line up with one another when the torque setting is about right. It's better to over-tighten to get to the hole to line up with the next space in the castle nut rather than loosen it to go back to another. Install a new split pin and you're done.

26. Pull the handbrake cable through the back of the drum and attach it to the lever, like so.

28. Fit drum, castle nut and new split pin. Don't forget to bleed and adjust the brakes and check for any signs of leakage.

8.4 Handbrake

The handbrake – also known as the parking brake or emergency brake in the USA – is an important piece of kit. It lives up to all three of the names listed above and should be checked and adjusted during your annual service, if not before, should you notice it's not as efficient as it once was.

How do you know when the handbrake requires adjusting? Simple. Sit in the car and, without pressing the button, pull the handbrake lever up towards you and count the clicks. If it clicks more than five times without making any noticeable difference to the car's brakes, it needs adjusting.

TOP: The handbrake is simple to adjust, but you must ensure your rear drums are properly set up before you start.

To adjust the handbrake you have to jack the rear of the car up and support it on axle stands. Check your rear brakes are correctly adjusted. If not, adjust them first and then pop inside the car.

Draw the handbrake cover back and you will find two cables with (ideally) two nuts on the end. Use a couple of 10mm spanners to slacken off the top nuts. You need to use a tight-fitting screwdriver in the slot to prevent the cable from turning.

Once both sides are loose, pull the lever up three clicks and then use the spanner to wind the bottom nuts down the cables, which tightens them.

Climb out and see if you can turn the wheels by hand. You should just be able to move them and they should have the same level of resistance on each side. Climb back inside the car and pull the lever up to its fourth notch. You shouldn't be able to turn the rear wheels at all now, which means the handbrake is properly adjusted.

Wind the lock nuts back down the cable to hold the lower ones in place, replace the rubber boot, and you're all set.

1. When the handbrake can no longer hold the car stationary, it's time for some adjustment.

2. The handbrake cable pulls on this lever to put the handbrake on.

8.5 Modifications/upgrades

Whilst there is not a huge amount wrong with a VW Beetle's stock braking system, there are a couple of things you can do to get the most out of it. So, before you go spending money, it's recommended you take a look at what you already have. What sort of condition are your brakes in and have they been maintained and adjusted as VW specified?

If everything is working as it should, a Beetle's drum brakes are more than capable of bringing one to a stop when the need arises. It's really only when you start upping the horsepower that you should think seriously about upping the braking performance to match.

That said, if you're only used to driving modern cars, a Beetle's stock drums can come as a bit of a shock. So, what can you do if you want to change things up with your braking game?

TOP: *Wave goodbye to adjusting and brake fade with a disc brake conversion, like this one from CSP.*

DISC BRAKES

These are the most obvious and commonly performed upgrade to a Bug's stoppers. The good news is that you can buy disc brake conversions for early Beetle-pattern wide five, late Beetle four-bolt and in Porsche pattern 5 × 130. Many owners take the opportunity to switch to discs when they decide to fit Porsche wheels. Obviously, it adds to the cost, but you are increasing the stopping power and you won't have to run adapters. Custom & Speed Parts (CSP) offers top quality kits for all of applications and are simple to fit. They are also German TÜV approved and have been rigorously tested over many, many years.

You can also buy rear disc kits, but suffice to say, you would upgrade the fronts to discs first, as you wouldn't want more stopping power on the rear than on the front. Having only discs on the rear would be like pulling the handbrake on, especially in the rain, but if you want the ultimate stopping power for a really hotted-up Beetle, then discs both front and rear are the way to go.

CSP disc brake kits are not the cheapest, but they have a well-earned reputation for quality.

DUAL-CIRCUIT CONVERSION

Beetles produced before 1967 came with single-circuit brakes. Whilst there is nothing wrong with that, what it actually means is that should one brake line fail, you lose all of your brakes. On the contrary, if you have dual-circuit brakes, the fronts or rears can fail, but you still have brakes at the end without the fault.

This is one safety measure every Beetle owner should consider even if they aren't converting to disc brakes. So, should you ever have a problem with your single-circuit master cylinder, don't buy a like-for-like replacement – take the opportunity to upgrade to dual circuit instead.

You will have to change the brake fluid reservoir and plumb in new hard lines, but everything you need is readily available and much cheaper than repairing bodywork damaged in an accident.

An original, single-circuit brake master cylinder.

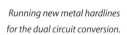

Running new metal hardlines for the dual circuit conversion.

A dual-circuit master cylinder with the reservoir mounted on top.

BRAKE HOSES

If you want to increase efficiency and reduce the chance of a spongy pedal, braided brake hoses are the way to go. That said, they are not strictly necessary unless you're a really spirited driver. However, what you *will* need are shorter front flexi-hoses if you're running a narrowed beam, as the stock ones will be too long. Stock hoses measure in at 470mm, but if you fit a 4-inch narrowed beam as on the featured car, then 1964–1966 flexi-hoses come in at 440mm, so are a much better fit.

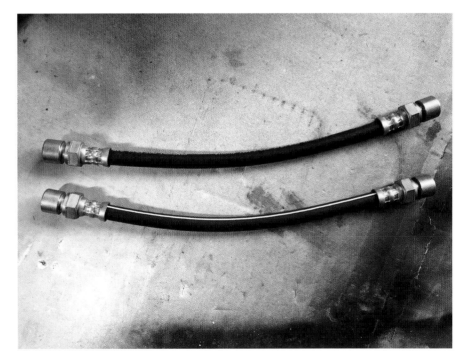

Original VW part number 211611701 is a better fit for cars running a narrowed beam.

TOP: *All Beetles, with the exception of 1302 and 1303s, have torsion bar front suspension like this.*

Suspension

9.1 Front suspension

With the notable exception of the MacPherson strut-equipped 1302 and 1303 models, all Beetles left the factory equipped with torsion beam front suspension.

What that essentially means is there are two metal tubes running across the front of the car, inside of which are sprung-metal leaf packs. There is a pin in the centre of both leaf packs to hold the leaf pack in place and another either side that the upper and lower trailing arms locate to. When you hit a bump in the road, the trailing arms go up and down, but the leaf packs resist the rotational effect

and return the trailing arms to their original position. This is how a Beetle's front suspension works and the great news is that it is rugged, reliable, easy to maintain and simple to work on. And, from the modifier's point of view, it has the added benefit of being easy to customize, once you know your onions.

REMOVING A FRONT BEAM

If you're reading this then there's every chance you might not even want to lower your car. Perhaps you want to return a modified Beetle to stock, or you just want to remove the front suspension to carry out some essential repairs. Either way, this is how you go about removing a front beam.

1. A piece of wood under the Napoleon's Hat section spreads the load.

Jack up

It goes without saying that you will have to raise the front end off the ground and support it in such a way that you can safely remove the beam. Chock the rear wheels, jack the front up and then support it on axle stands. A stout piece of timber placed on a couple of axle stands under the frame-head works well. Once you've lowered it down on these, give it a little rock to reassure yourself the car is properly supported and going nowhere.

Fuel tank

The petrol tank sits above everything you're about to work on, so it needs to come out. This is easier on an early car, as there are no filler neck tubes to remove and in the case of the 1958 featured car no fuel tank sender to remove either,

2. First things first, remove all the junk (and spare wheel) from your trunk.

as it has no fuel gauge. With the spare wheel and cardboard bonnet liner out of the way, you should easily spot the tank retaining clamps. Unbolt them and store all of the hardware somewhere safe. Lift the tank up enough to get your hands under and undo the fuel line. Remove the tank from the car and store it somewhere save. Drain the fuel into an appropriate container and think about maybe flushing and sealing the tank to prevent any dirt or rust particles getting into and clogging the fuel system in the future.

3. Remove the fuel tank clamps.

4. Disconnect the fuel line from the bottom of the tank.

5. An empty/light tank makes removing it so much easier.

6. Note the non-factory steering damper bracket. Early Beetles don't come with them.

Degrease

With the tank out of the way you can see what you are dealing with. Everything will be covered in muck and filth and some of the components will be reluctant to budge, especially if they have been on the car from new. The featured car's were cleaned off with a wire brush and some degreaser just to make it a little more pleasant to work on and then everything received a squirt of penetrating oil.

Weight loss

A complete front beam is a heavy old lump. You can remove them as a complete unit as shown, but it's much easier if you remove bulky items like the brakes and trailing arms to make working on your own less of a strain.

8. Leaking steering boxes are common, but you can rebuild them with new seals or buy a reconditioned unit.

Steering box

You can leave the steering box in situ for now, although removing it will lessen the load when you come to remove the rest of the beam; it's entirely up to you. The rubber donut is often split, so take a look at yours and order a replacement if necessary.

Tie rods

The front steering arms/tie rods run across the top of the frame head, so will have to come off to free the beam. They should have a castle nut and split pin holding them on, or if someone has already changed them, you may find nyloc nuts instead. Either way, remove them and then try to free

7. Removing as much weight as possible makes this job much easier.

9. Steering couplers and earth straps usually need replacing, but are an easy swap.

12. At the top, there is a shortened tie rod for a 4-inch narrowed beam and beneath it, a stock-width rod.

10. Separate the tie rods from the steering box pitman arm.

13. Place something underneath the flexi-hoses to catch the brake fluid that will inevitably trickle out.

11. Under all this muck and grease is a tie rod end that has to come off.

the tie rod ends from the steering box arm and spindles. You may get lucky and they simply pop out. If not, a whack with a hammer can be enough to shock them free. Alternatively, a ball-joint splitter is the tool for the job.

Brake hoses

The front flexi brake hoses need to be removed. There is a metal clip that slides over them on the frame head brackets and holds them in place. You can persuade them to come off with a hammer and large screwdriver and then wind them out of the hardlines with a spanner.

Beam bolts

The beam is now at a point where the only items preventing it being removed from the car are the six retaining bolts. There are two in the top of the beam and another four that go through the front frame head. They might be hard to see but VW installed metal lock plates behind the

14. A single-circuit brake fluid reservoir and two upper beam bolts.

15. Frame head bolts are longer than you think and can require a bit of effort to remove.

16. Slacken all four off and then remove the bolts one at a time.

17. Once down, wheel the beam out from underneath the car on the jack and marvel at VW's engineering excellence.

frame head bolts. They have little metal tabs bent around the bolt head to lock them in place. Use a fine screwdriver to push them back and then a larger one to bend the tabs far enough back to properly locate a socket or spanner on the head of the bolts. The bolts measure 19mm and you really don't want to round the heads off; they can be really stubborn to remove if they have never been off the car before. Crack them all loose and then place a jack under the beam to take its weight whilst fully removing them. The chances are the beam will need a little persuading to come out anyway, but don't take chances, as it is a hefty item that can do some serious damage if it falls on you.

Remove steering box

If you are not buying a complete replacement beam, spindle to spindle, you will need to remove a few more items. Start with the steering box. You'll find two further tab washers and castle nuts with split pins securing it in place. It's a good idea to take measurements of where it sat; that way you can take some of the guesswork out of bolting it to your new beam.

18. Measuring where the steering box sat on the old beam can take the guesswork out of fitting it to the new one.

19. Bend the tab washers back and remove the two 17mm nuts.

20. The greasy fudge all over the steering box means it has been leaking for some time.

21. Go any narrower than 2 inches and we doubt you will find anyone makes an anti-roll bar that fits.

Anti-roll bar

To remove the trailing arms, you will first need to remove the anti-roll bar. It's held in place by clips that need knocking off. Don't try to save them, as you will ruin them getting them off. Replacements are cheap and if you are going any narrower than 2 inches, you won't find an anti-roll bar to fit it anyway.

Trailing arms

With the front anti-roll bar out of the way, you can remove the trailing arms. They have a grub screw securing them to the end of the leaf packs that has a 19mm lock nut. Remove these and the arms should slide out of the beam with a little persuasion.

22. If you plan to reuse your anti-roll bar, you will still need to buy new fixings, as removing them usually destroys them.

23. These grub screws secure the trailing arms to the torsion bar leaves.

24. Spend a little time cleaning out the grub scrub so the Allen key fits securely. They are very easy to round out.

25. Ball joint-equipped trailing arms removed from a car.

Torsion leaves

In order to remove the torsion bar leaf packs you need to undo the grub screw in the centre of the beam. They will be filthy and difficult to manage, so place a cable tie around them and then wrap them in a bin bag or something similar to avoid smearing grease everywhere.

In order to run a narrowed beam you will need to cut them down and drill new dimples for the grub screws or buy a fresh set of leaves already cut to size. If your beam is 4 inches narrower than a stock one, you need torsion leaves and tie rods similarly shortened.

26. In these pictures you can clearly see the dimples that the grub screws locate in. One in the middle and one at each of the shock towers.

27. The central dimple that the beam adjuster locates in.

9.2 Rear suspension

If you have lowered the front of your Beetle, the chances are you will want to bring the back end down to even things out. Like the front, the rear end relies on torsion bar suspension. However, whereas the front end was designed to run at a specific, set ride height, the rear was completely adjustable, right out of the factory doors, requiring no additional parts or serious modifications to lower or raise it.

Simply put, the rear end has spring plates that attach to torsion bars (one per side) with a number of splines running around them. You pull the spring plate off the torsion bar and reposition it on the splines to adjust the ride height.

The torsion bars have a different number of splines at either end, with 40 on the inner end and 44 on the outer. Adjusting either the inner or outer or both sets of splines will have an effect on the ride height; hence, you will hear

VW people talking about how many inner and outer splines they have gone to lower their car.

Trying to work out how much each inner and outer spline change equates to in terms of ride height is enough to make your head swim. Fortunately, there are a number of online sites that list precisely this sort of information. The best is www.thesamba.com for anyone keen to know more about the dark art of rear spline alignment.

What you do need to know is that because there are fewer inner splines, if you rotate these it will have a bigger effect than adjusting an outer spline. You don't actually need to adjust both inners and outers, but doing so allows you to fine-tune your overall ride height.

LOWERING YOUR BACK END

Winding down the back a couple of clicks is a daunting task if you've never tackled it before, but like any job, actually doing it for yourself takes the mystery out of it and practice makes perfect. Also, no matter how many times someone

TOP: *A bit of nose-down rake, but the back has had to come down a couple of notches to level the ride height out a touch.*

1. You don't have to remove the rear drum, but you will see why some people do so in the next step.

3. Another shot of the rear with the drum removed, showing the handbrake mechanism.

has done this job, it's always a matter of trial and error. A Beetle's rear end tends to sag over the years and there are so many different combinations and variables of adjustment that nobody gets it right straight out of the box. Here's how you get started.

Jack up

Obviously you will need to raise the back end off the ground and support it securely on axle stands. You will also need to remove the rear wheel to give yourself some room to work, so whip that off now.

Handbrake

The cables need to be slackened off. You can either do this in the car at the handbrake lever by loosening the 10mm locknuts and adjuster nuts, or if you're going to be carrying out some brake work – such as converting the rear wheels from VW to Porsche pattern as here – then you can whip the drum off and remove the cable at the drum end. If you are going to remove the drum, then the car will need to be on the ground in order to remove the 36mm hub nut.

Rear shocks

Standard-length VW shocks are fine if you're only planning to drop the rear end a couple of inches; any more and you will need to replace them with shorter shocks. If you're not planning on replacing them, you can get away with just unbolting the lower mount and pushing the shock out of the way.

Axle tube nuts

There are three 19mm nuts and bolts that hold the spring plate to the axle tube. They're usually covered in decades of road grime, so you will need to give them a bit of a clean

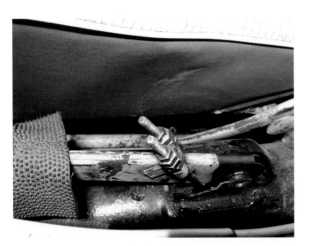

2. Slackening the handbrake off in the car is the easier option, but you can remove it from the drum if the rear end is stripped as shown.

4. You don't have to remove the rear shocks – just the bottom bolt should suffice.

5. Use a 17mm spanner on the nut and a 19mm socket on the bolt to remove the lower shock mounting.

up before a socket will slide securely on. They can be super-tight, so you will need a decent breaker bar to get them to shift. If no one has experimented with your suspension before, there should be a bump stop attached to one of these bolts. Depending on how low you plan on going, you will either need to trim the rubber down a touch or remove it all together. With them removed, you can slide the axle

6. These three spring plate bolts have to be removed.

7. A photo of what the bump stop looks like when fitted.

tube back off the spring plate and support it on an axle stand or an object of the right height.

Torsion bar covers

There are a couple of different designs, depending on the year of the car you are working on, but all are held on by three 15mm bolts. Again, they are usually covered in filth, so spend a few minutes cleaning them up to avoid rounding them off with your socket. You will find a rubber dough-nut inside. Pop that, the cover and the bolts to one side.

8. The spring plate cover needs to come off now.

9. With the cover removed you can see how the spring plate locates on the torsion bar.

10. The more reference points you give yourself, the better.

Spring plate

Now for a spot of risky business. The spring plate is under tension and removing it from the splines can be a little tricky. It's imperative you keep your hands and all other body parts out of the way as you lever it off the metal stop. It will go with a bang – especially if it's still sitting at stock height – and spring plates have been known to break the fingers and thumbs of those unfortunate enough to leave them in harm's way. Some people recommend coming at them from behind and hitting them with a mallet, but you do run the risk of knocking the torsion bar out of its housing and losing your original starting point. You should really try to avoid that, as it would be great to have a reference point of where you started and to be able to return to it if needs be. In fact, the best thing to do is to mark it in a couple of places before making any changes. Once it's free of the torsion bar, you can also mark the line of the spring plate on the torsion bar housing.

ADJUST HEIGHT

It's really just a question of how high or low you want to position the spring plate. Some people recommend using an angle finder to help set the spring plate height. They are certainly a handy reference tool, but most people just work by trial and error. And there can be quite a bit of that, as one side of the car might have sagged more than another over the years. Annoyingly, you won't know the height is where you want it, or equal on both sides, until you have bolted everything back together and lowered the car back on the ground. You need to roll it back and forth and allow the suspension to settle and then see what you think. Too much or not enough and you'll have to take another stab at it.

If you can get your head around one of the lowering tables dotted around the internet, the information they contain will at least give you some idea of the difference the inner and outer splines will make to lowering.

Basically, moving the spring plate one outer spline will move the spring plate by 8 degrees, or 2 inches. One inner spline will move the spring plate 10 degrees, or 2.5 inches. Therefore, a change of 4 degrees equates to 1 inch of lowering. For a 3-inch drop, you need to use a combination of inner and outer splines: rotate the rear by two inner splines (5 inches) and then raising it back up by one outer spline (2 inches). Hopefully that makes sense.

Go any lower than 4 inches and you will need to notch the spring plates to prevent it bottoming out on the upper stop. Or, fit a set of dropped spring plates, more of which in a moment.

It's also worth noting that when you drop the rear end 4 inches or more, you run out of toe adjustment at the end of the spring plate and this can lead to premature tyre wear. The solution to that is to run extended spring plates.

11. An angle finder can help if you have one, but setting the spring plate height is more trial and error than anything else.

12. You may have to take several stabs at this until you find the height you want. It's just that kind of job.

9.3 Modifications/upgrades

9.3.1 Front beam

Monkeying around with the ride height is the most common modification you will come across in the VW scene. Knocking a couple of inches out of your wheel arch gap might seem a bit silly, as it undoubtedly does compromise the ride quality and practicality of your car, but it does look good.

TOP: *The '58 project car runs a lowered and 4-inch narrowed link pin beam with 4.5-inch replica BRM wheels.*

Beetle beams come in two distinct flavours, link pin and ball joint and both are modified in the same manner.

All Beetles built prior to August 1965, for the 1966 model year, have link pin front suspension. After that they switched to ball joints, the belief at the time being that ball joints were cheaper to manufacture and required less maintenance than the old king and link pin set up. Sadly, that proved not to be the case as the rubber boots perish and the joints prematurely wear out.

It is a commonly held belief that link pin cars can run lower and drive smoother than a ball joint car at the same height, to which you also need to install long travel ball joints to prevent them binding up.

Skinny tyres alone won't see your car rolling low, and there are a number of other ingredients you need to chuck into the mix if you want a lowered Bug.

LOWERING AND NARROWING

The most common beam modifications are lowering and narrowing. The first is pretty self-explanatory. Owners lower their cars to tighten up the handling and for the aesthetic appeal. Truth be told, it's mostly for the latter, as a low Beetle looks cool, but it's a modification that is not without its drawbacks.

Narrowing is precisely that. Many owners remove the stock-width front beam and replace it with a narrower one. Why on earth would anyone want to do such a thing? Again, it comes down to visual appeal for the most part. Tucked in wheels and a skinny front end is *de rigueur* in the VW scene simply because it looks good. This is obviously a matter of personal opinion, but there is also some method in this apparent madness, as by tucking the wheels in further you can run lower, as it creates extra clearance for the front wheels.

Some owners only want to narrow their front end enough to accommodate upgrades such as wider wheels and tyres or dropped spindles and disc brakes, which increase the track-width and can push the wheels out enough to rub on the wheel arch lips. Other owners take it to the extreme and go as low and narrow as possible. Believe it or not, you can chop as much as 10 inches out of a beam, but not without significant modifications.

If you are only looking to tuck a wider set of alloys and disc brakes under the front end, a 2-inch beam will suffice. Arguably, the most commonly fitted narrowed beam measures in at 4 inches narrower than stock. They are readily available from any number of specialists and a 4-inch beam gives the desired look without requiring any bodywork modifications. Go any narrower and you will find yourself having to modify things like the inner wings or running without shock absorbers, which is a serious deviation from stock and something your local MoT inspector would take issue with – if you still take your MoT-exempt Beetle for a test, that is.

It's a case of horses for courses – and modifications of this nature come with a multitude of pros and cons. The pros are that it means you get a cool-looking car that can run seriously low. The cons are a reduced turning circle, less ground clearance, lots of work and expense and no matter how good the engineering behind the products you are using may be, or what anyone would have you believe, your car will no longer drive in the way that VW intended.

The beam in the front of this photo is the stock-width beam as removed from the car featured in this book. The one behind it is the 4-inch narrowed beam that it was replaced with. Four inches is a fairly tame amount of narrowing by today's standards, but still requires a certain amount of effort to fit.

You can see the difference in width here between a stock and 4-inch narrowed beam.

Beam adjusters

The beam that was removed was not entirely a stock component. It has had adjusters welded into the centre of the tubes to allow the ride height to be lowered or raised back up. These adjusters replace the central grub screw that pins the leaf pack in place. The adjuster has a slot that allows the grub screw to be twisted up or down, raising or lowering the position of the trailing arms. There is a block-and-lock nut that allows you to fix the adjuster in the desired position.

The budget option in the past was simply to cut out the centre section and weld it back in with the grub screw in the desired position. Welding an adjuster in instead is so much better though, as it allows you to fine tune the ride height. If you want to go low, you need a beam with adjusters.

Adjusters are exactly that: they allow you to change the position of the leaf pack and, therefore, the ride height.

If you want a skinny front end on your Beetle, the beam has to go on a diet.

End plates

A lot of the width removed from a beam comes from replacing the beam end plates and shock towers. In this photo you can clearly see how much thinner they are on the new beam that was fitted. They also don't hang down as low. Beams with end plates that protrude an excessive amount bellow the bottom tubes are apt to smack the ground and wear away on really slammed cars.

Skid plates

You don't actually need one of these, but they are a sensible option in a world of madness. Installing a skid plate on the bottom of your beam will protect the lower adjuster bolt. On really low cars these often come into contact with the ground and wear away. The skid plate protects it but there

This skid plate only tasted a few miles to end up like this. The car was probably too low, so it was raised up a little.

With and without. It is better that the skid plate takes this sort of punishment than the car itself.

are two schools of thought here. First, they're a great idea and protect the underside of your car. Second, if you didn't have a skid plate hanging a couple of centimetres below your front end, it wouldn't hit the ground in the first place. Nonetheless, some people fit them just so they can watch sparks fly.

ANY OTHER BUSINESS?

Yes. Whenever you do anything to your suspension that may alter the tracking, you should have it checked and reset if necessary, by someone who knows what they are doing. If you don't, you'll have a car that handles terribly and munches its way through tyres.

Depending on how low and narrow your car is, you won't be able to take it to just any tyre-fitting centre to get the tracking looked at. They won't be able to get under the arches to hang their measuring equipment. What you need is a really old-school garage with a set of traditional Dunlop gauges like these. You will also need a flat floor to work on and the know-how to use the equipment.

Finding a garage to set the tracking on a really low Beetle isn't easy, but it is vitally important you do so.

9.3.2 Dropped spindles

They might sound like something from your grandma's sewing box, but dropped spindles are a key ingredient for running low. They are the components that the front drums attach to and as the name suggests the spindle portion sits at a different height to a stock spindle. It actually sits 2.5-inches higher, which has the effect of raising the wheels 2.5-inches in the front arches and lowering the front end by the same amount.

What's great about dropped spindles is that they are a simple bolt-on job and don't require any other beam modifications or shorter shocks. Better still, they don't affect the ride quality in any way, as they retain full suspension travel.

For someone looking for a mild reduction in ride height they are the perfect solution. For all those looking to slam their car to the max, they're an absolute must, as they drop the car by a couple of inches and then you can go the rest of the way with the beam adjusters.

The downside to dropped spindles is that they increase the front track width. That is not a problem if you're running stock wheels and tyres, but add a wider alloy and possibly some after-market disc brakes and you are likely to need a narrowed beam to tuck everything back in again. A 2-inch beam would do the trick.

The likes of Custom & Speed Parts (CSP) in Germany offer CB Performance spindles for both link pin cars and later ball joint-equipped Beetles and for both drum and disc brake applications.

TOP: *Dropped spindles for an early link-pin beam.*

Dropped spindles raise the wheel up by 2.5 inches, thus dropping the front of the car by the same amount.

The beam on the left is fitted with standard spindles, the one on the right has 2.5-inch dropped spindles. Can you see the difference?

CSP-supplied dropped spindles will lower your car but not affect the ride quality, if anything, they will tighten up the driving experience.

9.3.3 Spring plates

If you have read the chapter on adjusting rear suspension, you will already have some appreciation of what's involved with getting the back end of a Beetle to sit just right. You can only do so much with stock rear spring plates and lowering the back end of a swing-axle Beetle can lead to some sketchy handling at times.

Dropped spring plates like these from EVA Resto (www. evearesto.co.uk) raise the back wheels up by 2 inches when installed in the original factory position, but the angle of them allows you create a much wilder drop, depending on how you set them on the splines.

They also do away with the need to notch the spring plate if you go for more than a 4-inch drop and they clear the factory suspension stop, which means you have decent suspension travel when running low.

Specifically engineered to allow correct wheel alignment, you won't prematurely wear through your rear tyres like

you would with a factory spring plate and the long adjuster screw allows you to really fine tune the finished ride height. They are a fantastic addition to any modified Beetle.

TOP: *Dropped and adjustable spring plates for a swing-axle Beetle, made by EVA Resto.*

The angle of these dropped spring plates has been designed to clear the upper bump stop when running low.

Install these in your stock location on the splines and you will still have a 2-inch drop but none of the drama.

The adjuster block allows you to fine-tune the final ride height.

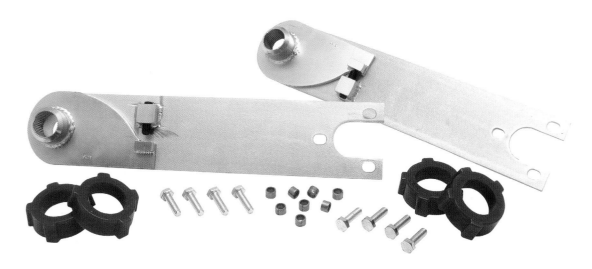

CSP supplied Sway-A-Way adjustable spring plates offer 1.5-inches of up or down adjustment and come with new urethane bushings and fittings.

9.3.4 Air ride

Whilst a slammed Beetle arguably looks great, the reality is a car with zero ride height is a pain to live with if you actually want to drive it anywhere. Speed bumps become mountains to climb, curbs become no-go zones and even getting off your drive can result in some serious scraping.

But what do you do if you want a crazy low Beetle that you can actually drive? The answer is simple even if the

TOP: *Two Beetles with very different ride heights – one stock and one as low as you can go, thanks to air ride.*

work involved is not. Put it on air. Having a Beetle with air suspension gives you the best of both worlds, as it means you can have a really low car but the ability to raise it up at the flick of a switch when the need arises.

Some people only have air at the front so they can raise the nose of the car enough to get over obstacles; others go the whole hog and fit it front and back so they can have even more control of how their car sits.

Air-shocks can provide a super-comfortable ride – but the more air in them, the firmer they become and the harsher the ride becomes. As such, most owners set the car

This Mexican Beetle runs an air-management system. Here you see it at a practical driving height.

Here it is again at full drop. Air ride allows you to transform the look of your car at the flick of a switch.

to where they want it to sit – i.e. low – and then only have to pump a little air in to make the ride stiffer or softer.

Fortunately, those so inclined can now buy full air-ride kits from any number of sources that can be fitted at home. However, changing VW's tried and tested suspension for something entirely different can be a little daunting, so there are specialists like Max Edwards at EVA Resto (www. evaresto.co.uk) who can sell you everything you need and then install it for you. Getting your car in the weeds has never been so easy, but there are too many things to cover here that will be specific to your car and how you want it to look and handle, so rather than a step-by-step guide, here is just a brief overview of what's involved.

HOW DOES IT WORK?

To put it simply, you are replacing a Beetle's fixed-position torsion bar leaves with circular through-rods that are free to rotate up and down, thus moving the trailing arms in the same manner. This is achieved by replacing the standard oil-filled shock absorbers with air shocks, or a combination of air and oil. Air is pumped into the bags on the shocks via an air-tank, filled by a compressor that is activated by switches inside the car. The more air you pump into the shocks, the higher they raise the car; the more you let out, the lower the car sits or returns to the lowest point it was set at. It's pretty simple when you think about it.

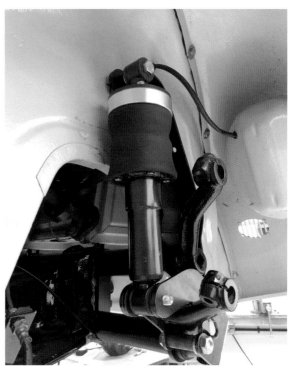

This is what all the fuss is about. Replacing the front shocks with air shocks allows you to alter the ride height at will.

A full front-end air ride installation from EVA Resto.

This shot shows how far you can raise the front wheels. The front wings will literally rest on the tyres or the chassis will sit on the floor, depending on how it's set up.

What do I need?

Luckily, the likes of Max at EVA have done the hard part for you and come up with bolt-on kits for both link pin- and ball joint-equipped Beetles. You will need to change your front beam for one of their custom-built 2-inch or 4-inch narrowed beams, some of their Free Roll rods that replace the torsion bar springs, some air shocks, shock mount relocators that allow the shock to operate within its full range of movement, correct length steering rods and a steering extender/quick steer kit. You will also need to run some 2.5-inch dropped spindles to run seriously low.

One of EVA Resto's air-ride front beams. Note the round through-rods protruding from the beam's end plates.

AirSleeve shocks are the components that actually raise and lower the height of the car.

Shock relocators do exactly that – they place the air shock in the optimum position to provide the maximum amount of lift.

Air management

You need some form of air management system to be able to direct air to the shocks and regulate how much is going in and coming out at any one time. You will also need to install an air-tank to hold a ready supply of air and an air compressor to fill it back up again when it empties. The number of compressors and the size of your air-tank will affect how quickly the system operates. The smaller the tank, the less air you have to play with and, when it runs out, you have to wait for the compressor to kick back in again and fill it enough to give you some more lift. You need a system that manages all of that and enables you to control it at the flick of a switch or tap of your Smartphone.

The more you spend, the more functions you have to play with, and the top of the range kits have programmable ride height pre-sets that raise the car on start-up to your pre-determined ride height.

You don't have to spend a lot and many people go for the more budget-friendly four-way Paddle Valve Management kits. There is no computerized control/display, but manually controlled valves to raise and lower the car.

Everything in this car is controlled by an Airlift 3P Complete Digital Management Package. It's not cheap, but it is very clever.

Hide the air tank away or make a feature of it. The choice is yours, but the larger the tank the more functionality you have.

What about the rear end?

EVA also offer their own premium bolt-on kit that mounts to the frame horns. It comes with all the mounts, stiffener bars, air-bag brackets, shock relocators and extended spring plates you need to get the back end seriously low. Comprehensive installation guides are included with all kits and EVA can provide all the information you could possibly need to get your car literally sitting on the ground.

Complete bolt on air-ride kits are available for the rear and, being bolt on, can be removed as well to return a car back to stock.

ANY DRAWBACKS?

Of course there are drawbacks. For a start you are altering the factory suspension – something VW invested vast sums of money in designing and developing. There is also the added expense of the kit, the job of fitting or paying someone else to fit it, and you need to make room for things like the compressor, air tank, controls and running the air lines. You increase the risk of something failing on your car, such as an air line popping off, which could leave you stranded with a car sitting squarely on the ground. However, the flip side of the coin is that you get killer looks and controllability. One minute you can have your car laying frame on the road, the next you can be driving over a speed bump. At the end of the day, you pay your money and make your own decision based on the information available. If you don't want air-ride, nothing anyone is going to say is going to convince you otherwise and vice versa.

A car as low as this isn't for everyone, but if it is, there is a lot of quality kit available off the shelf and ready to bolt on.

9.3.5 Wheels and tyres

There is more to how a car looks than the suspension alone. The cool kids like to call it 'stance' and it's entirely a matter of personal opinion. Some owners like their cars to be scraping the ground, others like a bit of nose-down, bottom-up Cal Look rake, others like their car to be entirely stock.

No matter what your personal preference, your Beetle will never sit right if you don't give a little thought to the wheels and tyres you are fitting. Simply put, the wrong wheel and tyre combo can ruin the overall look of any car, no matter how much time, effort and money you've invested in the restoration. So what should you be thinking about?

WHEELS

These are the obvious place to start, as they make the biggest difference to how your car will look. Whilst there is

TOP: *Building a cool car is about the entire package. Everything needs to work together and complement one another, but it all comes down to personal preference.*

absolutely nothing wrong with the stock steel wheels and hubcaps your car left the factory with, a cool set of alloy wheels really lifts a car's appearance. They also come in wider sizes than the factory-fitted steels, so you can run fatter tyres for more grip and road presence. If you want to do that but keep a stock look there are any number of specialists out there who are ready, willing and able to widen (band) your original wheels.

Most modifiers opt for something skinny on the front, like a 4.5-inch wheel, that keeps the steering light and allows a decent amount of tuck and lowness. For the rears, you have a bit more space to play with, so 5.5-inch or 6-inch wheels and chunkier rubber are the norm.

What style should you go for? That's for you to decide and the best way to do that is to wander around a VW show and see what others have fitted to their car. Most Beetle owners are more than happy to talk about their car and will tell you how to go about fitting something similar to your car.

There are loads of wheel options out there, at a range of different price points. Original, period wheels will

This modern take on the EMPI five spoke has a standard early VW wide 5 × 205 bolt pattern.

A replica of the iconic Porsche wheel, the Fuchs comes with a Porsche 5 × 130 bolt pattern.

The 5 × 205 Enkie.

Originally a Porsche offering, these Cosmic alloys now come in both Porsche and VW wide-5 bolt patterns.

The 5 × 205 Sprintstar.

cost a premium and budget wheels don't tend to last very long in the UK climate. A good mid-way point in terms of price and quality would be the offerings from CSP in Germany (www.csp-shop.com) and a few of the most commonly-fitted styles they offer are shown in the images here.

Bolt pattern?

Which wheels to fit depends a great deal on the year your car was made. All Beetles sold in the UK up to 1967 had the 5 × 205 bolt pattern. All German-built Beetles after that come in 4 × 130 and if you want to run Porsche-style alloys, like the Fuchs or Cosmic, they come in 5 × 130, so you will need to change the brakes to match the bolt pattern or run adapters.

5 × 205 to 5 × 130 adapters are the budget way to run Porsche wheels on an early VW. The best way is to fit Porsche-pattern brakes.

TYRES

Believe it or not, these are as important as the wheels you fit. Too fat or too tall and you will run into clearance issues and they will look all wrong. There is an increasing trend amongst purists to go back to the cross-ply tyres that VW fitted back in the day. Whilst these are period-correct, they can lead to slippery handling in the wet, which is why the world moved on to radial tyres many years ago.

To get the front end as low as possible and really accentuate the narrowness of their front beam, most owners fit a skinny front tyre and then run something much larger on the back. Historically and when there wasn't as much choice as there is today, owners would run a 145 R 15 or 135 R 15 Firestone or Michelin. These were produced for the likes of the Citroën 2CV but were found to be ideal for a mildly dropped Beetle.

Things have moved on since then and cars have become even lower – hence, you see a number of old-school Beetle modifiers running 125 R 15 Firestones on their front wheels.

Whilst there is no denying they look right, a 125 will feel super-slippery in the wet and can lock up when braking, especially if you're running after-market disc brakes.

Cal Look aficionados won't like this, but times have moved on from those too. Nowadays, most people running a lowered Beetle run what are commonly known as Smart car tyres. These are so-called because they were designed for the tiny Smart car of a few years back. Something like a modern 145/65 R15 or a 135/70 R15 is perfect for a 4.5-inch alloy bolted to a 4-inch narrowed beam and whilst they have a lower profile than a Firestone or Michelin, they have a larger contact patch on the road. Hence, when it came to choosing new rubber for the black '58 Beetle shown throughout this book, a modern 145/65 R15 was the tyre of choice.

Our project car is fitted with 4.5 and 5.5-inch replica BRMs in a standard 5 × 205 early VW bolt pattern.

For tyres it was opted to run 145/65 R15 on the front and 195/65 R15 on the back. However, the rears will probably be changed for something a little meatier in due course.

10

Electrics

There are many things you can do to a VW Beetle's electrical system to make them more reliable and/or wrangle a few extra horsepower out of one. Simply replacing a few of the tired, old or worn-out components can make more difference than you might imagine. But what can you do to winkle the bugs out of a Bug's electrics?

WIRING

Let's start with the wiring loom. There are thousands of Beetles still running around with their factory-installed wiring looms. The problems set in when owners begin splicing in additional wires to fit things such as modern radios or to bypass faults they can't get around the correct way. (That is, tracing it back to the root cause and fixing that.)

TOP: *Poor wiring leads to poor running, so it's best to investigate further to avoid future issues.*

The term 'rat's nest' is fitting when it comes to a lot of Beetle wiring, but you don't have to replace the entire loom to make a Beetle happier, simply deleting any additional wires that shouldn't be there and checking, cleaning and tightening-up the connections is an afternoon well spent. Fuses corrode, wires break, and earths forget what they are there for – and any one of these faults can lead to serious issues.

At the very least, you should certainly inspect any non-factory looking connections to see how well, or not, they have been attached. And, checking everything is properly connected and working as it should will help you understand how everything operates and spot faults when they do arise.

Coil

How to upgrade to electronic ignition has been covered elsewhere in this book, but there are other things you can

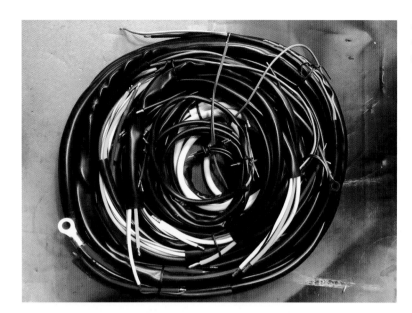

Replacement looms are available for Beetles of every year. This one is from Wolfsburg West and comes with detailed fitting instructions.

For a vintage look, a lick of paint and period-style stickers can disguise any make or budget coil, as shown.

opinion. Some say they are unreliable, others say they don't make any difference.

Distributor

An incorrect or worn-out distributor can lead to poor running. You can rebuild your existing distributor, pick up a used replacement at a swap meet or buy a reconditioned one from a specialist. Modern replacements get bad press on the internet so again, do your research, consider your options and buy whatever ticks your boxes. The replacement engine in the car featured in this book didn't come with a distributor, so it was decided to try one of the vintage-style cast iron distributors from Kuhltek Motorwerks. With its Bakelite cap it has the period looks required and has the same ignition curve of a Bosch 009 with 22 degrees of advance. Only time will tell if it was money well spent or if it will be necessary to track down a decent original.

A modern replacement distributor with points and condenser set-up, although you can also buy a fully electronic version.

do to take things a little further. Basically, the fatter spark you can generate the bigger the bang you get. A fatter spark allows you to run a wider spark plug gap, which gives you more power, a smoother-running engine and better fuel economy. So, whilst there is nothing wrong with a good old-fashioned Bosch coil, that's just it – it is merely a good old-fashioned coil – and there are better-performing options on the market, such as the Flamethrower coils from Pertronix. The Flamethrower coil is supposed to deliver 15 per cent more spark energy than a regular coil but, like electronic ignitions, they divide

A Custom & Speed Parts (CSP) alternator conversion kit.

Alternator

Whilst there is nothing actually wrong with a stock VW generator, swapping it for an alternator is a good move if you want to run accessories such as additional spotlights, larger stereos and amplifiers. Alternators are an improvement because they deliver higher amps at a more consistent rate, whatever the rpm, whereas a generator barely charges at all when the engine is idling. Many alternators come with an internal regulator and fitting them is easy; just a few wires to change and the pedestal it sits on.

HT leads

When was the last time you replaced your spark plug wires? Pretty much all of the cars the author has ever bought have come with an ancient set that have become stiff and unmovable. A replacement set can be had for as little as a tenner, but where is the fun in that? Instead, the author decided to give his 30-bhp engine some period-style, braided HT leads and made his own for the same price as a halfway-decent set of modern replacements.

Don't underestimate the difference that something as simple as a fresh set of HT leads can make to an engine.

Some braided leads were found online and a set of old Beru leads was cannibalized for the ends in order to make these old-school HT leads for the 30bhp engine on the project car.

It's often the little details that make the biggest difference to how a project turns out.

Braided hoses come in regular cloth finish or with a clear protective sleeve. Buy the latter or you will rue every mucky finger print.

Paint and Bodywork

11

When the project car featured in this book first arrived, it was obvious it had not been shown any love for quite some time. The lustre had entirely gone out of the black and it looked more like blackboard paint than the usual quality offering from Wolfsburg. The bonnet had also been hand-painted and there was a rough coating of surface rust on the roof.

However, don't be fooled into thinking that just because a car looks a little tired on the outside you will necessarily have to fork out for a repaint. A decent exterior re-spray does not come cheap and is not always necessary.

If you are willing to invest a bit of time and effort you can genuinely work wonders on faded, original paint with the only real cost being the purchase price of a machine polisher and some cutting compound.

TOP: *Purchased online, this polisher cost around £50 and came with a selection of polishing pads.*

The paint applied at the factory is robust stuff and, dare we say it, a lot better quality than some of the stuff people replace it with.

Don't be mistaken: if you want a show-quality paint job that turns heads then there are tons of reputable body shops out there that will be happy to oblige, but if you follow the process explained here, you might discover you really don't need to bother and save a fortune in the process.

It is also worth pointing out something that appears to be peculiar to the VW scene. That is, a huge amount of owners would rather have a car with faded, original paint than a fresh coat of shine that could be hiding a multitude of sins and shoddy repairs underneath. In fact, hard as it is to believe, a great many people will pay a premium for a car still sporting original paint – even more so if it has a bit of character or 'patina'.

Whatever your views on the matter, a car is only original once and it is always preferable to preserve a car's history rather than simply whitewashing over it. Once it's gone, it's gone forever.

'Mopping' a car – so-called because you use a Machine Operated Polisher – is not a particularly dark art, but a lot of people are put off having a go because they have heard how easy it is to burn through the paint. Whilst you do run the risk of burning through, if you take your time and use some common sense you should be fine. And, what's life without a little risk? Fortune favours the brave as the old saying goes.

So, the following process is definitely worth a go if you love the idea of preserving patina or are simply looking to save a few pounds whilst saving up for a re-spray further down the line.

2. Don't bother leathering off or removing streaks from the glass at this point. You will see why in a minute.

PRESERVE AND PROTECT

Image 1 (below) was our starting point. A number of patina fans said they would have left it alone but we wanted to see if the dull, flat paint could be made to shine again. Looking round the car it was evident that the paint on the main body shell, doors and deck lid was original, but the wings had been repainted or replaced and were sufficiently thick to risk the polisher.

1. The project car has lots of character with all its chips and dents, but a polish would breathe new life into it.

THE POLISHING PROCEDURE

Body wash

The first step is to give the entire car a thorough wash. It is always worth giving any new (to you) car a thorough clean before you do anything to it; that way you will go over it in detail and spot anything that needs doing and decide on your plan of action.

Test spot

Pick an area to start on. Ideally, you should choose an inconspicuous spot to see how you go. On the featured project car, the author dived straight into the bonnet, which is arguably the most noticeable part of the car. It had been crudely brush painted at some point in its past but it was evident there was still good paint lurking beneath.

3. If you have areas like this on your car, you really have nothing to lose by having a go yourself.

Preparation

To do the job properly you should remove as many pieces of trim as possible. Items like the side trim, headlights, bumpers and anything that prevents you making a clean sweep with the polishing machine.

Wet sand

If your paint is just flat and a little tired you can skip this stage, but the car featured in this book had the aforementioned brush-painted bonnet that needed tidying up and lots of surface rust and imperfections. Hence, the bodywork was given a light, wet sand with 2000 grit paper. This gets rid of minor imperfections and will smooth out the

4. Use plastic trim-removal tools, not screwdrivers, to avoid damaging any paint and trim that you are removing.

6. You can use a block but it's easy to burn through the paint on radiused areas and there are lots of those on a Beetle.

this, the paper will create scratches in the surface and more work for yourself.

Go easy

Stop from time to time and clean/dry off the area you are working on. You will be able to both see and feel the results

5. Use coarser 1000 grit paper to break through any badly applied brush paint, as here, but go easy and keep an eye on how things are progressing.

paint surface; the smoother the paint surface, the better results you will get.

Soapy water

Keep dipping the paper into a bucket of clean, soapy water. The soap and water prevent the paper clogging up and helps it glide over the surface. Change your water regularly to avoid transferring dirt back onto the car. If you don't do

7. Go easy and keep checking your work.

8. All of the brush marks seen in step 3 have been removed at this point.

9. A polisher makes for light work, but you will need to tackle any smaller areas – such as swage lines and vents – by hand.

as you go as the surface becomes smoother. Don't get too carried away. It's easy to rub through to the primer below the topcoat – especially if the car you are working on is very old and the paint very thin.

Smooth operator

When you are happy the surface is smooth enough, drop down to finer grades of wet and dry. 2000 grit does the job, but you can also achieve a decent result with 1200 and 1500 grit; it just depends on the paint on the car you are working on. Black cars, like the one featured in this book, really show up scratches and imperfections, so going as far as a 6000 grit paper will really smooth it out.

Cutting it fine

At this point, your paint will look flat and horrible – but it's about to look a whole lot better. What product you use is down to you, but Farecla G3 cutting compound is recommended. A little goes a long way and machine polishing is a messy business. You will get polish all over you and any area you are working on, so cover up anything you don't want covered in splatter.

Stay local

Apply the cutting compound to the panel you are working on. You don't want it to dry out so try to go no larger than 50cm (20in) square – perhaps even less if it's a hot day. You want a good, even, but not too thick or thin layer to work with.

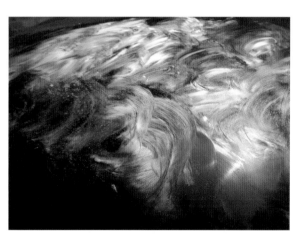

10. Too much polish and it will flick everywhere; too thin and the polisher will dry the compound out and it will not be as effective.

QUICK RESULTS

The results speak for themselves. Compare this to how the bonnet on the featured car started out. The trick is to take your time and develop a feel for what you are doing. You will need to make several passes and don't worry about the mess you're making – that's all part of the process. Buffers generally have variable speed settings. Original paint is tough so can handle a higher speed setting, whereas newer paints tend to be softer and easier to burn through. Start out on a slower setting and speed up as you go. You can also wet the area or the polishing pad to help avoid burning through. Hold the buffer at an angle so just the front edge of the pad comes into contact with the car. Work the

11. Wet sanding revealed lots of character, but there is now lots of shine, too.

machine back and forth, up-and-down and side-to-side. Don't linger on one spot for too long and if you are in any doubt, stop and if needs be tackle that area by hand.

Rough spots

The other area that was really bad on the featured car was the roof. Not only did it look bad, but thanks to all of the rust staining, you could also feel how rough the paint was by running your hand over the surface.

A step backwards

Simply repeat the previous steps with the wet and dry, using a high grit to break down the worst of the surface imperfections before going down to a finer grit for a smoother finish before buffing.

12. Remember, the more you sand and polish, the more paint you will remove – so go easy, or you will soon be down to primer or bare metal.

13. Soak the paper in water to soften it and fold it over to help your grip. Curled edges and dirt on the paper will create scratches.

14. It's not perfect, but it is a lot better than when it was started.

Rust removal

Make no mistake, you do need to put some effort into this task, but it is definitely worth it. How much better does the roof look after only using the wet and dry? Admittedly, some of the black, factory paint has been removed and the roof has been given some more patina, but a smoother overall finish has been created and the rust has gone. This is often the case with rusty paintwork. It looks like there is a lot of corrosion when in fact there is just a larger bubble of rust sitting on a small imperfection in the paint. Knock the head off the rust and then apply a coat of wax to stop it coming back.

Added character

After a couple of passes with the polisher the author was certainly happy with the results. The bumps, lumps and

15. VW people will often pay a premium for an OG (original) paint car like this.

surface staining were gone, and there was some really characterful patina on the shiny roof.

Buff and wash

This is definitely a messy job – the residue and splatter get everywhere. Once you have gone over a section with the polisher you should use a good, clean cloth to buff the surface and remove as much of the remaining compound as possible. Once it is buffed, you will need to give the car another wash. Hose it down until the water runs clear and there is no milky residue. To stop the paint from dulling down again you will need to apply a good quality wax. You can use your new-found skills with the MOP or do it by hand if you fancy working up a sweat.

16. Original VW paint is robust stuff and can look amazing with a little work and a lot of mess.

HAVE A GO

Compare the starting point to the almost finished car. 'Almost finished' because there was still a lot of work to do before this car hits the road again and it would get very dirty and dusty in the garage, so the plan was to come back and polish it again before driving it. However, having a clean and cool-looking car in your garage is inspiring. It

made the author want to get out and work on it and see it finished and on the road. It also really only cost the price of the polisher and a free afternoon, so was definitely time and money well spent.

As it was bought: dull, flat and looking a bit unloved.

After a few hours with the wet and dry and polishing mop. If your paint work looks tired, what have you got to lose?

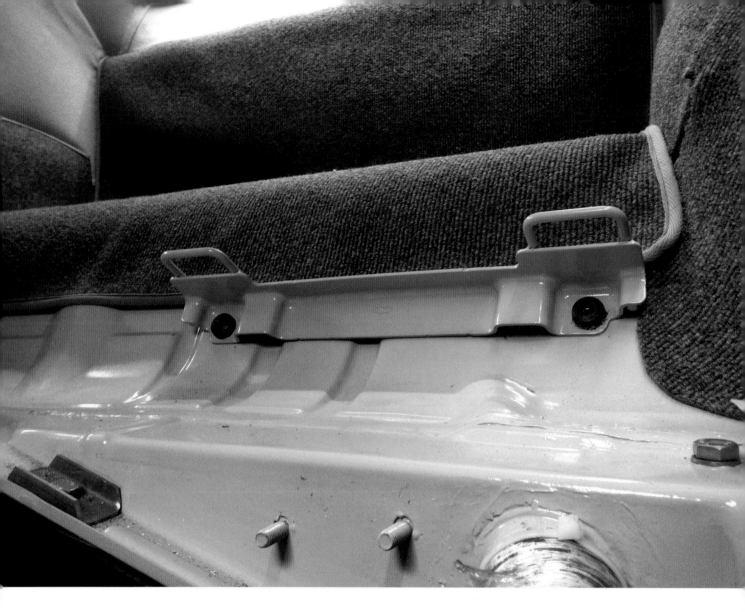

12

ISOFIX

In the event of an accident, Beetles don't exactly inspire confidence. It is fair to say that vehicle safety has moved on somewhat since the Beetle was first conceived. At best, the early Beetles came from the factory with three-point belts in the front and, at worst, no seatbelts at all. Impact protection in Beetles is non-existent and, if you are unlucky enough to have an accident, the only crumple zone is likely to be your face.

So, what do you do if you want your young family to come with you as you Beetle about?

ISOFIX

Modern cars now come with ISOFIX, which is the international standard for attaching child safety seats. It automati-

TOP: ISOFIX is the safest and easiest way to install child seats in a car. But in a Beetle? How?

cally locks a car seat, or car seat base into place on fixed metal attachment points.

One of the many beauties of ISOFIX is that you can hardly see the mount once it's fitted. Due to the way this one is installed, when the car seat isn't in use, it can be removed and everything looks factory-original again.

Another point to bear in mind is that you can get ISOFIX seats and booster seats that will accommodate a child until they are old enough to start wearing lap belts. And when that happens, you can simply take the retrofit mount out and use the holes to fit lap belts without the need for any more drilling.

Obviously, no Beetle left the factory with ISOFIX, so this is a modification that not everyone will be keen on. Also, a word of warning: if you are going to attempt this on your own car, you need to use common sense and take responsibility for your own work. The area you are mounting the bracket to needs to be structurally sound and you must use proper fixings. Lives depend on it.

1. The mount comes painted black, but this one was colour-coded so that it wouldn't stand out against the upholstery.

What you need

Believe it or not, the part you need is actually a Ford item. It's a retrofit mount made specifically for older models of Fiesta. It costs a little over £15 and is a well-made and strong looking mount.

Spreader plates

This mount is only going to be effective if correctly fitted – and to good, strong metal. In the event of an accident you don't want it to pull through the bodywork and, to avoid that, you need some spreader plates. Whilst it might not be as strong as a new, factory fitted ISOFIX system, it is certainly safer than no restraints at all. You could take things a step further by welding retaining nuts to the plates for added security. The thinking here is that it will prevent the nut from vibrating loose. The plates are located between the body pressings and won't be able to turn so by welding the nut to them, they won't become loose either.

Measure twice

Drill once, as the saying goes. Although you should measure as many times as it takes until you are 100 per cent happy with the position of the mount. Use tape to mark the holes you need to drill, a punch to stop the drill bit from slipping and then make your holes.

2. Spreader plates are 2.5 × 2.5-inch 5mm steel plates with an M12 bolt hole.

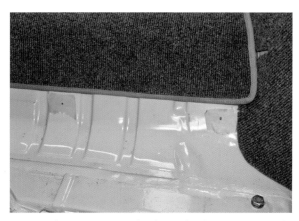

3. You must be 100 per cent sure that the metalwork you are mounting the bracket to is totally solid.

4. Check you are not drilling into anything important. There should not be anything behind there to damage, but you never know.

Another pair of hands

You will require the assistance of a helper at this point, as one of you needs to slide under the car to position the spreader plates while the other bolts the mount through the car. A coat of seam sealer will keep the elements out and a locking nut on the back of the mounting bolts isn't a bad idea, either.

5. Here are the spreader plates, painted up and with a little sealer applied to prevent water getting behind them and entering the car.

6. Installing the spreader plate is an awkward business, but the end result is worth a little discomfort.

Stealth and safety

With the rear seat fitted you can see how the mount sits between the seat base and back. They are hardly noticeable and when your kids are big enough for seat belts, you can remove the mount and use the holes for belts.

7. A neat installation – and a very useful one at that.

With the rear seat installed the brackets are hardly noticeable.

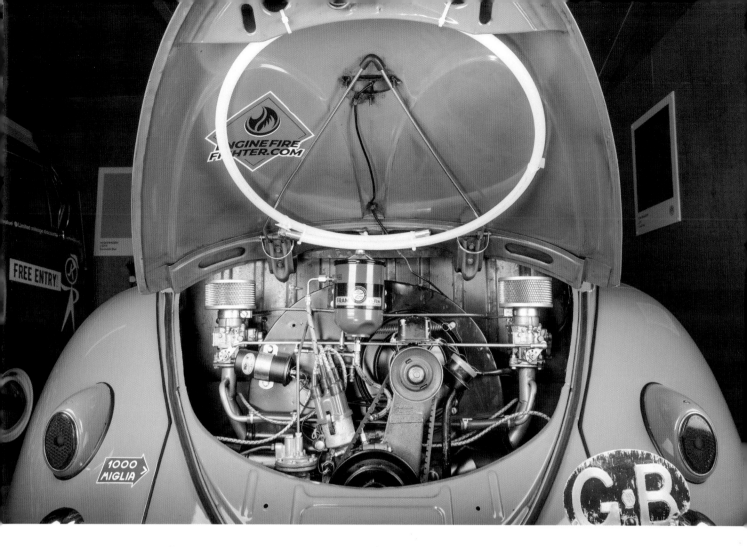

13

Fire Suppression

Engine fires are a major concern for all Beetle owners. Fuel lines perish or pop off, allowing fuel to drip onto hot surfaces or the distributor, leading to the inevitable and worst-case scenario – a fire. Most owners don't realize there is a problem until they see smoke pouring from the rear end and, by then, it's usually too late to do anything about it.

This why you should always carry a fire extinguisher inside your car, although an automatic fire-suppression system mounted in the engine bay is a more effective weapon against engine fires.

Just Kampers (www.justkampers.com) stock the one shown here, which is called an 'Engine Fire Fighter'. It is basically a 2-metre, pressurized flexible tube filled with a non-corrosive, non-toxic agent that leaves no residue behind if it is called into action.

You use cable ties to fix it to the deck lid and it will go off automatically should the temperature reach 120 degrees Celsius. Clever stuff and well worth investing in one.

TOP: *An automatic extinguisher like this can stop a fire in its tracks and is money well spent.*